D1216398

The
Connell Guide
to
Mary Shelley's

———

Frankenstein

———

by
Josie Billington

Contents

NOTES

Introduction

"There never was a wilder story imagined," wrote one reviewer on the first publication of *Frankenstein* in 1818: "we do not well see why it should have been written" (*The Edinburgh Review*, 1818). The admiring Sir Walter Scott felt that *Frankenstein's* "unexpected and fearful events... shook a little even our firm nerves" (*Blackwood's Edinburgh Magazine*, 1818).

The novel, capable of producing almost visceral shock and terror in its unprepared readers, was the work, more surprisingly still, of a young woman of 18 who would describe herself later in life as one who was "not for violent extremes" and apologise for her tendency from childhood to "hang back" out of a "horror of pushing, and inability to put myself forward". The puzzle is not *why* the novel was written: the question, "so very frequently asked me", as Shelley herself said, is *how* it came to be written: "How I, then a young girl, came to think of and to dilate upon so very hideous an idea?"

That Mary Shelley would write *something* was never in doubt. The daughter of two of the most celebrated radical writers of the Romantic period, William Godwin and Mary Wollstonecraft, and the wife of the genius poet, Percy Bysshe Shelley, her "literary reputation" – as the Preface to *Frankenstein* explains – was more or less the project of her husband, as it had been of her father. Moreover, the novel was written amid circumstances of unusually rich creative inspiration. Mary and Percy spent the summer of 1816 in Switzerland, living next to the poet Lord Byron on the shore of Lake Geneva. Confined by incessant rain during a stormy season, the group's custom was to read and talk late into the night at Byron's villa. One evening, during this "casual conversation", Byron proposed: "We will each write a ghost story." *Frankenstein* was thus conceived.

For all the idiosyncratic uniqueness of its literary influences and origins, the enduring power of the story could never have been anticipated. Indeed, as the first work of an inexperienced writer, its cultural legacy is extraordinary. "It's a commonplace now that everybody talks about *Frankenstein*, but nobody reads it," wrote the critic George Levine in 1979:

> Of course, *Frankenstein* is a minor novel,
> radically flawed by its sensationalism... But it is
> arguably the most important minor novel in
> English... We can hear echoes of it, not only in
> Gothic fiction, science fiction, and fantasies of all
> sorts, but in far more "respectable" works, written
> before the glut of cinematic distortions.
> *Frankenstein* has become a metaphor for our own
> cultural crises.

The prophetic power of the novel's imagery in reflecting the dehumanising effects of science, technology, empire, business and the mass media has never abated. Writing in 2002, Jay Clayton said:

> As a cautionary tale, *Frankenstein* has had an illustrious career; virtually every catastrophe of the last two centuries – revolution, rampant industrialism, epidemics, famines, World War 1, Nazism, nuclear holocaust, clones, replicants and robots – has been symbolized by Shelley's monster. Perhaps more than any other novel, *Frankenstein* has been interpreted as a warning about impending events.

For some readers these warnings have produced a monstrous creation *in place of* Mary Shelley's own. *"Frankenstein* is a product of criticism, not a work of literature," argues Fred Botting.

Yet if the metaphorical interpretations of the novel appear to exceed the adolescent fantasy which gave rise to them, this is in itself a tribute to the original work, concludes Levine: "The book is larger and richer than any of its progeny and too complex to serve as mere background... The novel has qualities that allow it to exfoliate as creatively and endlessly as any important myth."

A summary of the plot

Robert Walton, an Englishman on a journey to discover a passage to the North Pole, writes a series of letters to his sister describing the treacherous sea voyage. In them, he recounts how, when the ship became stranded on all sides by ice, the crew witnessed a being of gigantic stature in the shape of a man, crossing the ice on a dog sledge. The following day, the crew take on board a frail, exhausted and frozen man, whose own sledge has drifted toward the ship on a fragment of ice. The man is Victor Frankenstein, whose pursuit of the creature has brought him thus close to death.

As Frankenstein recovers, he tells his incredible history to Walton. The eldest child of loving parents, Frankenstein grew up in Geneva, with his adopted sister Elizabeth, and his younger two brothers, William and Ernst. Victor's youthful imagination is fired by the fanciful scientific philosophies of the ancients and especially by their pursuit of the elixir of life – the key to immortality. He is also fascinated by contemporary theories of electricity and galvanism. Before Victor leaves home to pursue his scientific studies at the University of Ingolstadt, his mother, Caroline, dies of scarlet fever, expressing as her last wish that Victor and Elizabeth will marry.

At University, Victor is inspired by his teachers to an obsessive pursuit of chemistry. For two years, he devotes himself to unceasing study, day and night, seeing neither family nor friends, until he discovers the secret which had eluded science until this moment: the "cause of generation", "the principle of life". With this power at his disposal, he succeeds on one fateful night in bringing to life a creature of his own fashioning. Instead of the beautiful creature he has envisaged, however, the creature's appearance is repulsive and Victor instinctively flees from it in horror, barely noticing that "one hand was stretched out, seemingly to detain me". The creature disappears, Victor is struck by a feverish illness in which he loses his senses, and is nursed slowly back to health by his childhood friend, Henry Clerval.

When news arrives from Victor's father of his brother William's murder, Victor hastens to Geneva. In the woods where William was strangled, he espies his creature, and is immediately convinced

THE MANY MYTHS OF *FRANKENSTEIN*

The truth of a myth, as Lévi-Strauss rightly insists, is not to be established by authorizing its earliest version, but by considering all its versions. The vitality of myths lies precisely in their capacity for change, their adaptability and openness to new combinations of meaning.

That series of adaptations, allusions, accretions, analogues, parodies and plain misreadings which follows upon Mary Shelley's novel is not just a supplementary component of the myth; it *is* the myth.

So writes Chris Baldick, one of several critics who have traced the myths which grew up around Mary Shelley's novel during the 19th century. *Frankenstein*'s influence is found in representations of working-class resistance in Victorian times as the rising up of a fearful monster. It is found equally in

that it has killed his brother. Arriving home, however, Victor finds that an innocent young girl, Justine, beloved of the family and adopted by it, stands accused as the murderer, having been found with the locket (bearing a picture of his mother) which William was wearing on the night he died. When Justine is tried and executed, Victor's guilt at the cause of the deaths of these "innocent loved ones" is as profound as it is lonely, since he feels no one will believe his story.

Seeking to ease his grief, Victor sets off for the mountains. There he encounters his creature, who proceeds to tell his own sorry tale. Eloquent and learned, the creature explains that after leaving

---

Karl Marx's characterisation of oppressive capitalism and machine technology in *The Communist Manifesto* as an alien and demonic power, "an animated monster".

So widespread is *Frankenstein's* influence within 19th-century fiction, that its legacy is not only palpable in the transgressive "dualist" fantasies of the late Victorian period – Robert Louis Stevenson's *Dr Jekyll and Mr Hyde* (1886), Oscar Wilde's *The Picture of Dorian Gray* (1891), Bram Stoker's *Dracula* (1897) – and in the "mad scientists" of H. G. Wells's science-fiction creations: *The Time Machine* (1895), *The Island of Dr Moreau* (1896), *The Invisible Man* (1897). Its impact is felt as well in the iconic portrayals of Victorian women and orphaned children who are abandoned, maltreated, deprived: Pip in Charles Dickens *Great Expectations* (1861), Jane in Charlotte Brontë's *Jane Eyre* (1847), Jude Fawley in Thomas Hardy's *Jude the Obscure* (1894).

George Levine goes so far as to say that Mary Shelley's novel provided the model or "pattern" for all 19th-century realist fiction: Frankenstein is

Victor's workshop and finding himself shunned by mankind, who fled from him in terror, he took refuge in the wilderness. Living hidden in a hovel, adjacent to a family, the de Laceys – who, he comes to understand, are also outcasts from society – he learns from their loving ways, as well as indirectly from their conversation and their books, how to read and write. Though the sight of his reflection in a pool has revealed to him his horrific appearance, so acute is his longing for companionship that he approaches the family nonetheless, hoping that they will see beyond his disfigured body to his human need for love.

But on sight of the creature the family take flight

---

the "indirect father" of later protagonists who "reject the conventional limits imposed upon them by society and are punished more or less for their troubles": Becky Sharp in William Thackeray's *Vanity Fair* (1847–8), for example, or Lydgate in George Eliot's *Middlemarch* (1871–2).

For Chris Baldick, *Frankenstein's* impact is evident well into 20th-century Modernism too, notably in Joseph Conrad's apocalyptic myth of over-reaching imperialism, *Heart of Darkness* (1899), in which the tale of the "factitious god", Kurtz, is

offered via a series of embedded first-person narratives, as well as in D. H. Lawrence's embodiment of the "world-conquering will of the British industrial bourgeoisie" in his portrayal of the entrepreneur Gerald Crick in *Women in Love* (1920). This is aside from *Frankenstein's* influence on literature in Europe – the transgressive *Tales of Hoffman*, for example – or the way it is echoed in that monumental struggle of man and creature in America's most famous 19th-century myth, Herman Melville's *Moby Dick, or The Whale* (1851). ∎

from their home in mortal fear. Hurt and enraged by their rejection, he destroys their cottage and garden and vows revenge on mankind and especially his creator. The murder of William, and the implication in this act of Justine (with whom the monster himself had left the locket while she was sleeping), are the reflex, the creature says, of his suffering, sense of abandonment and forlorn loneliness. He pleads with Frankenstein to create a female mate for him so that he, too, can enjoy companionship and happiness, promising that if Victor grants his request he will disappear from human sight.

Victor is at first moved to compassion by his creature's argument, and, accompanied by Henry Clerval, he sets out first for England in preparation for his task, and thence to Scotland where he and Henry separate. Secluded in the Orkneys, he begins creation of a female only to be struck with alarm that he will be unleashing a new breed of monsters to afflict the human race. When he finds his first foul creation watching his work through a window, he destroys his second before it is completed. Enraged, the monster vows to be with Victor on the night of his forthcoming wedding to Elizabeth. Frankenstein disposes of the remains of the female creature in a lake only to be arrested on suspicion of murder when he arrives on shore. The victim is his friend, Henry Clerval, who has been strangled by the monster. Imprisoned, Victor suffers another breakdown. He eventually returns to Geneva with his father on being acquitted.

Victor marries Elizabeth soon afterwards and on their wedding night, fearing the monster's sworn revenge, he sends Elizabeth to their room, while he seeks the monster's whereabouts. When he hears Elizabeth screaming, he realises that his wife, and not himself, is the intended victim. His father, stricken with grief by the deaths of so many loved ones, also dies. Bent on revenge, Victor pursues his monster to the North Pole. In a dog sled chase, he almost catches up with his creature, but the sea beneath them swells and the ice breaks, leaving an unbridgeable gap between them. At this point, Walton encounters Victor, and the narrative catches up to the time of Walton's fourth letter to his sister.

When the ship becomes packed with ice, Walton and his men have to abandon their voyage and head homeward. Victor, whose health has steadily worsened, dies soon afterwards. Walton finds the creature on the ship, hanging over Victor's body, in agony of grief for the loss of his creator and struck with remorse for the suffering he has caused him. Vowing to end his suffering in death, the creature disappears into the darkness.

What is the novel about?

As Chris Baldick says, what *Frankenstein* is "about", at one level, requires only two sentences:

(a) Frankenstein makes a living creature out of bits of corpses.

(b) The creature turns against him and runs amok.

Yet this "skeleton", as Baldick also says, has given rise to all kinds of "interpretative elaborations".

One reading, among the almost inexhaustible number the novel has generated, sees *Frankenstein* as being "about" Mary Shelley. Taking its cue from her complex literary heritage, this reading treats the novel as a disguised autobiography, variously expressing: Shelley's experience (as daughter, wife, mistress, mother and writer); her psychological resistance to aggressive male mentors, and the damage they did to her, politically and artistically; and an anti-rational dream vision or nightmare produced in reaction (involuntarily or consciously) to her father's intellectual emphasis on mankind's capacity for reason.

Other critics find this view too narrow and too personal. They see the figure of Frankenstein's monster as reflecting the fundamental questions – social, moral, political and metaphysical – which were provoked by the French Revolution of 1789, questions which remain unresolved in our current age. Mary Shelley created an image irresistible both to her own culture and to ours because it says so much about the shift towards a secular world – about the passing of power and values from God to man. This is why the great secular thinkers of modernity (Darwin, Marx and Freud and their intellectual offspring) are frequently invoked in discussions of this wild and improbable horror fantasy.

It is worth recalling, however, what the novel itself claimed to be "about" when first published, albeit in a Preface written by Percy Shelley (1818). He wrote that however the behaviour or "moral tendencies" of the characters might affect readers, the story itself was chiefly concerned with "the exhibition of the amiableness of domestic affection, and the excellence of universal virtue".

Percy Shelley may have been seeking to pre-empt the accusation that the novel is "unladylike" by stressing its "feminine" concerns, but it is hard to quarrel with his view, and it's hard to find a critic who does. The keynote is struck very early in the novel, in Walton's "frame" narrative. Walton writes to his sister:

I have no one near me, gentle yet courageous, possessed of a cultivated as well as of a capacious mind, whose tastes are like my own, to approve or amend my plans... It is true that I have thought more and more that my daydreams are more extended and magnificent, but they want (as the painters call it) *"keeping"*; and I greatly need a friend who would have sense enough not to despise me as romantic, and affection enough for me to endeavour to regulate my mind. (Letter 2)

For Mary Poovey, it is a founding tenet of the novel that individual appetite "can and must be regulated – specifically by the give-and-take of domestic relationships". This thesis is supported by the fact that the following dialogue between Walton and Frankenstein was substantially added to by Mary Shelley for the 1831 edition of the novel. "I spoke," says Walton of his first encounter with Frankenstein, "of my desire of finding a friend, of my thirst for a more intimate sympathy with a fellow mind than had ever fallen to my lot, and expressed my conviction that a man could boast of little happiness who did not enjoy this blessing":

> *"I agree with you," replied the stranger [Victor Frankenstein]; "we are unfashioned creatures, but half made up, if one wiser, better, dearer than ourselves – such a friend ought to be – do not lend his aid to perfectionate our weak and faulty natures."* (Letter 4)

Frankenstein's creature might be seen as a perverse, distorted fulfilment of the fantasy of having in one's life, as Walton puts it, "the company of man who would sympathise with me, whose eyes would reply to mine" (Letter 1). Certainly, one of the greatest surprises for readers who encounter the novel for the first time, with experience hitherto only of its cinematic distortions, is that this ghoulish horror story is, on some level, really "about" the virtues of friendship.

What kind of novel is *Frankenstein*?

In 1816, Mary Shelley set herself to write a "ghost story" – one which, she said,

> would speak to the mysterious fears of our nature and awaken thrilling horror – one to make the reader dread to look round, to curdle the blood, and quicken the beatings of the heart.

For many readers, *Frankenstein* is the archetypal Gothic horror tale. The period of the classic Gothic novel is usually thought of as beginning with Horace Walpole's *The Castle of Otranto* in 1764 and ending more or less with Charles Maturin's *Melmouth the Wanderer* in 1820. Published in 1818, *Frankenstein* falls squarely into this period.

The novel's Gothic credentials are powerfully self-evident. A mysteriously brooding atmosphere of gloomy grandeur is felt from the first pages where the vast, inhospitable landscape – wild, impenetrable, isolated, unknown, majestic, threatening – is succeeded in later chapters by

Cover illustration from a late 19th century edition of Frankenstein

secret machinations in ghostly burial chambers and unholy work in a dark, remote garret that is no less alienatingly obscure and menacing. Violent ambition and mad ravings, unlicensed desire and unbridled excess, share centre stage with monsters and skeletons, diabolic creations and life-threatening pursuits, supernatural evil and criminal villainy. The whole is an enticing mix of terror and suspense, revulsion and excitement, strangeness and marvel.

Yet *Frankenstein's* real affinity with the Gothic tradition is not its trappings but the backlash it represents against the values of a previous age –

those of 18th-century Enlightenment, or the Age of Reason. Emphasising Greek-classical restraint in its art, and rational consistency in its thought, the Enlightenment had made life everywhere susceptible to human control. The world was no longer strange or uncertain – inaccessible in its secrets – as it had once been. It was complete and knowable, and existed to meet the needs of an exalted human civilisation.

While this rationalism was secure and safe, it was also lacking in energy and wonder. Reasoning with life, one did not fear it. The Gothic, therefore, was a revival of interest in all that was antique and elemental, raw and basic. It expressed and satisfied a primal need for the grandeur of spiritual mystery – what Edmund Burke called the "sublime" – in place of the mediocrity of finished perfection. As

THE SUBLIME IN
FRANKENSTEIN

"The Greek art is beautiful. When I enter a Greek church, my eye is charmed and my mind elated... But the Gothic art is sublime." The notion of the sublime was a cherished concept of the Romantics and, as Coleridge's eulogising definition makes clear, indissolubly related to Gothic as a genre. The founding text of the sublime was the work of the conservative Romantic, Edmund Burke, *A Philosophical Enquiry into the Origins of Our Ideas of the Sublime and Beautiful* (1757).

Whatever is fitted in any sort to excite the ideas of pain, and danger... whatever is in any sort terrible... is a source of the *sublime*; that

David Punter puts it in his classic work on the genre, *The Literature of Terror:*

> Where the classical was well ordered, the Gothic was chaotic; where simple and pure, the Gothic was ornate and convoluted: where the classics offered a set of cultural models to be followed, Gothic represented excess and exaggeration, the product of the wild and uncivilized... Gothic was the archaic, the pagan, that which was prior to, or was opposed to, or resisted the establishment of civilized values and a well-regulated society... [Gothic] primitivism and barbarism possessed a fire, a vigour, a sense of grandeur sorely needed in English Culture.

is, it is productive of the strongest emotion which the mind is capable of feeling. I say the strongest emotion, because I am satisfied the ideas of pain are much more powerful than those which enter on the part of pleasure... [Pain] is always inflicted by a power in some way superior, because we never submit to pain willingly.

It is towards the sublime "magnificence" of the "terrifically desolate" Alpine regions that Victor Frankenstein turns after the monster has destroyed the lives of those he loves, as the only scene commensurate with his woe:

> The weight upon my spirit was sensibly lightened as I plunged yet deeper in the ravine of Arve. The immense mountains and precipices that overhung me on every side, the sound of the river raging among

Radical *un*reason, silenced in the preceding century, was suddenly liberated into fantastic art.

Yet, in so far as Gothic was an ideology as much as a literary genre, it was only a more brazen and violent version of the literary movement to which it was most closely allied – Romanticism, itself a reaction against Enlightenment restraint. Gothic was but one symptom of a shift of emphasis from decorum to imagination, from complacent stability to ambitious idealism, which was the essence of the Romantic disposition.

"The Gothic," writes Marilyn Butler in *Romantics, Rebels and Reactionaries,* is a product of three generations of quickening pulse, the revolutionary era from about 1760 to about 1789. With its "motifs of isolation and suffering", the Gothic had a "diverse potential" for Romanticism's radical political

---

the rocks, and the dashing of the waterfalls around, spoke of a power mighty as Omnipotence – and I ceased to fear or to bend before any being less almighty than that which had created and ruled the elements, here displayed in their most terrific guise. (9)

Frankenstein experiences "a sublime ecstasy that gave wings to the soul and allowed it to soar from the obscure world to light and joy" (10). His state repeats Percy Shelley's "trance sublime and strange" in his poem of tribute to the selfsame landscape, "Mont Blanc'", written in the same year and same place as *Frankenstein.* As in Shelley's poem, where Mont Blanc's magnificence is "rude, bare and high,/Ghastly and scarred and riven", "hideously... heaped around" by ice and rock, so nature, in *Frankenstein,* is more terrible than consoling, more indifferent than benevolent. ∎

messages. The images of Gothic characteristically "project an evil and disturbing environment":

> Though no specific moral need be pointed concerning the corruption of the present order or the desirability of rejecting authority, the subliminal frame of reference is felt to be breakdown of control, both in the psyche and the state.

The early Gothic novelists were not themselves political radicals, Butler points out; rather, they used the genre to give free play to private and public extremes of vision which were in conflict with cultural norms.

But Mary Shelley's Gothic tale was enmeshed in – literally, married to and born of – Romantic radicalism. She was the wife of one of the leading lights of the Romantic movement, Percy Bysshe Shelley, and the daughter of two of its originators, William Godwin and Mary Wollstonecraft. The "politics" of Gothic are arguably nowhere more potent than in *Frankenstein*.

In fact, *Frankenstein's* relationship with the wider Romantic movement explains why, in some respects, the novel is remarkably *un*-Gothic. There are no castles, no monasteries, no churches, no abbeys. Mary Shelley's "ghost" story does not contain any supernatural elements at all in the conventional sense. The laboratory replaces the looming Gothic ruin, and scientific experimentation the malevolent scheming of the villain-hero. Above all, *Frankenstein* is not set in the remote medieval past, but in a modern present, breaking altogether with the Gothic's association with retrospection and nostalgia. In this way, as Fred Botting has pointed out, *Frankenstein* can be seen as revitalising a genre whose fire was burning out and adapting it to the needs of modernity.

For this novel engages directly with the pressing issues and events of the real world in which it was written. If traditional writers of Gothic ignored the upheavals wrought by the industrial and French revolutions, Mary Shelley's novel does not, embracing rather the implications of a changing world. Indeed, as her 1831 Preface explains, the novel was inspired by cutting-edge scientific thinking – "the nature of the principle of life, and whether there was any probability of its ever being discovered and communicated". In that momentous summer of 1816, Lord Byron and Percy Shelley talked of the experiments of the physician and natural philosopher, Erasmus Darwin (grandfather of Charles Darwin):

> Dr Darwin... preserved a piece of vermicelli in a glass case till by some extraordinary means it began to move with voluntary motion... Perhaps a corpse would be reanimated; galvanism had given token of such things: perhaps the component parts of a creature might be manufactured, brought together and endued with vital warmth.

Frankenstein is the first science-fiction tale in so far as it is based on experimental thinking which takes it beyond the existing boundaries of science. What Mary Shelley says of her novel's subject might readily be applied to the novel itself: "Invention consists in the capacity of seizing on the capabilities of a subject..." (Preface, 1831).

Yet it was also horror at what *might* be invented which inspired this enduring tale. Frankenstein's creature raises fundamental questions about the proper limits not only of scientific endeavour, but of human activity itself. The first sci-fi novel is also, as Northrop Fry says, a gripping "precursor of the existential thriller" – a story uncannily modern in its concerns, not least in the way it raises challenging questions about how we live in a secular world.

Ultimately, this novel refuses to be contained by genre – which is one reason it has spawned so many (often incompatible) interpretations. Like the monster whose story it relates, the tale has a life and meaning beyond the intentions of its own creation.

Who is telling the story?

You will rejoice to hear that no disaster has accompanied the commencement of an enterprise which you have regarded with such evil forebodings. (Letter 1)

This is the opening sentence of *Frankenstein*. The language of extremes ("rejoice", "disaster"), as well as of risk ("enterprise", "evil"), is one which we might expect to belong to the story's protagonist-hero, more especially since the narrating voice is speaking in the first-person.

But this is the voice not of Victor Frankenstein, but of Robert Walton, writing to his sister, Mrs Saville, at home in London, while starting out on a treacherous voyage of discovery to the North Pole. In a series of four such letters, Walton recounts meeting, in this "seat of frost and desolation", a wild and despairing Frankenstein, who – almost mad and almost dead – is thus wretchedly at the end of his own adventure. "Chapter 1" of the novel begins when Frankenstein tells his own tale, retrospectively, in his own person.

But why doesn't the novel simply begin at the beginning? One clue lies in Frankenstein's prefatory remarks to his narrative:

Prepare to hear of occurrences which are usually deemed marvelous. Were we among the tamer scenes of nature I might fear to encounter your unbelief, perhaps your ridicule; but many things will

appear possible in these wild and mysterious regions
which would provoke the laughter of those
unacquainted with the ever-varied powers of nature.
(Letter 4)

The introduction of these marvellous occurrences within Walton's letters back home to his beloved sister strategically defends the story against the reader's "unbelief" or ridicule. The letters are a bridge between the "wild and mysterious regions" into which Frankenstein's tale gives access, and the conventional and familiar middle-class society to which the tale's Gothic matter is opposed. In many ways, the anonymous and silent "Mrs Saville" is the reader's proxy, hearing a tale related with eye-witness convincingness which, nonetheless, she would find implausible and incredible were it not told to her by someone she trusts – by "one of her own". Robert Walton has much the same function in *Frankenstein* as does Mr Lockwood in Emily Brontë's *Wuthering Heights,* grounding strange and improbable events and characters within commonsensical, ordinary, "real life".

In fact, in formal terms, *Frankenstein* is a model for Brontë's later Romantic novel. Like *Wuthering Heights,* the narration proceeds as if by a series of Chinese boxes: from Chapter 1, Frankenstein's story nests inside Walton's; from Chapter 11, the monster's tale nests inside Frankenstein's. Within these narratives, there are multiple smaller ones belonging to mothers, sisters, friends or casualties who are affected by the catastrophe. At the conclusion, the novel resumes Walton's "outer" or framing narration as part of the return to reality and matter-of-fact normality. In this way, as George Levine has pointed out, the anarchic energies and nightmare qualities unleashed by the book are contained within a tight, restraining structure.

But these multiple stories are never hermetically sealed one from another: the novel's restraining form also sets up a kind of echo chamber so that the action occurring in one tale recalls or comments upon what has happened in another. These nested first-person narratives generate rich allusive resonances. We are put on notice to expect mirrors and parallels when, even before Frankenstein begins speaking, Walton says of him: "My affection for my guest increases every day. He excites at once my admiration and my pity to an astonishing degree... I begin to love him as a brother... as the brother of my heart" (Letter 4). As Barbara Johnson puts it: "The teller is in each case speaking into a mirror of his own transgression."

Another important feature of Shelley's narrative mode is the Romantic way it privileges first-person, subjective accounts rather than relying on a controlling, omniscient narrator. The primary aim of the Gothic novelists, says Robert Kiely in *The Romantic Novel in England*, was not to depict real life and manners:

Their preoccupation [was] with the subjective

nature of reality and their commitment was to [the] imagination... The subjective vision became the crucial event... external reality paled before it or fused with it, but never dominated it.

The expression of "subjective reality" was one of the ways that Gothic violated taboos:

The Gothic novel was a deeply serious attempt to break through old conventions and to probe areas of experience not approached by the preceding generation... [It] explored feelings and compulsions which were not merely impolite to mention but often difficult to label.

"I cannot describe what I then felt," says Victor Frankenstein, when the loyal servant, Justine, is condemned for the murder of Victor's younger brother at the hands of his own creature. "The torture of the accused did not equal mine; she was sustained by innocence, but the fangs of remorse tore my bosom and would not forgo their hold" (8)*. The monster's subjective experience is offered as an "excuse" for his cruel offences in the external world. In explanation of his brutal deeds, the monster says:

I was forever deprived of the delights that such

---

* The numbers in brackets throughout this guide refer to the chapters from which the quotations are taken

beautiful creatures could bestow... the joy-imparting
smiles... on all but me... Can you wonder that such
thoughts transported me with rage?" (16)[*]

The fact that these experiences are offered in the absence of a controlling narrator means that the novel never has to endorse or condemn them. Indeed, for Mary Poovey, in her famous feminist essay on the novel, the narrative structure is a means of deliberately avoiding responsibility for any one point of view. It is an evasive strategy, symptomatic of Mary Shelley's ambivalence towards artistic expression when – in an era in which a woman was expected to conform to a conventional model of propriety – being a writer at all could be in conflict with social acceptance.

> Because of [the novel's] three-part narrative
> arrangement, Shelley is able to create her artistic
> persona through a series of relationships rather
> than a single act of self-assertion; and she is freed
> from having to take a single definitive position on
> her unladylike subject. In other words, the narrative
> strategy of *Frankenstein*, like the symbolic
> presentation of the monster, enables Shelley to
> express and efface herself at the same time.

This abrogation of responsibility is also consonant with Mary Shelley's claims that the original inspiration for her story came to her from "far beyond the usual bounds of reverie... My imagination, unbidden, possessed and guided me, gifting the successive images that arose in my mind... I saw – with shut eyes but acute mental vision... the hideous phantasm" (Preface, 1831).

Yet if Shelley's narrative method is a way of meekly hiding behind her creation, another important effect of the novel's structure, says Anne K. Mellor, is "to slow down the narrative, allowing time for extended meditations by both the creature and Frankenstein on the nature of morality, the responsibilities of God and parents, and the very principle of life itself".

What these concentric meditations also yield, moreover, is a richly inconclusive thought-experiment. As George Levine puts it:

> The novel's elaborate clarity of structure... does not reflect a firm moral ordering but a continuing complicating diminishment of [reality]... The language keeps reinterpreting itself, reaching for that community of understanding that allows us to posit a truth. But satisfaction does not come... In the end we are not left with a judgement.

The power of this form and of this myth, for George Levine, is its radical refusal of closure: it is impossible to pin down exactly what it means. This is as true of its philosophical as of its political stance, argues Pamela Clemit: "The drama of revolutionary struggle takes place in a subjective account which assigns the task of evaluation to the reader."

Is Victor Frankenstein a hero?

I may there discover the wondrous power which attracts the needle and may regulate a thousand celestial observations that require only this voyage to render their seeming eccentricities consistent forever... I may tread a land never before imprinted by the foot of man. (Robert Walton, Letter 1)

...success shall crown my endeavours... Why not still proceed over the untamed yet obedient element? What can stop the determined heart and resolved will of man? (Robert Walton, Letter 3)[*]

The world was to me a secret which I desired to divine. Curiosity, earnest research to learn the hidden laws of nature, gladness akin to rapture as they were unfolded to me, were among the earliest sensations I can remember. (Victor Frankenstein, Chapter 2)

My mind was filled with one thought, one conception, one purpose. So much has been done... more, far more, will I achieve... I will pioneer a new way, explore unknown powers, and unfold to the world the deepest mysteries of creation. (Victor Frankenstein, Chapter 3)

The language of heroic enterprise dominates the first quarter of the novel. It is the key point of contact not only between Frankenstein's narrative and Walton's but between the novel and the whole ideology of individualist endeavour which had founded the Romantic movement. Indeed one way of reading this novel is as a moral-philosophical enquiry into the nature and ambitions of the Romantic movement, especially as, for some critics, these ambitions were represented by Mary Shelley's husband, Percy Bysshe Shelley.

Some details suggest that Shelley may have provided one model for the novel's protagonist. "Victor" (Frankenstein's first name) was one which Shelley used for himself as a child. Both Frankenstein and Walton are associated with the creative impulse of poets – whose "effusions", says Walton, "entranced my soul and lifted it to heaven. I also became a poet and for one year lived in a Paradise of my own creation" (Letter 1). (As Harold Bloom points out, though, it is actually Victor's friend, Henry Clerval - composer of songs and tales, "deeply read" in "the virtues of heroes" and "occupied with [the] moral relations of things"- who is "rather more like Shelley".) Clearly, however, Percy Shelley is not just written into the novel, he is central to its very conception. With his "passion for reforming the world" and his "mad enthusiasm" for science (chemistry in particular), he "provided the subject" of *Frankenstein*, says Christopher Small.

The novel's subtitle, *The Modern Prometheus*, is the essential clue to his influence. Prometheus, the Greek fire-God of classical legend, rebelled against the presiding deities of Mount Olympus by stealing fire from the Gods to give to humankind. It was virtually the gift of life itself, for which Prometheus suffered the eternal punishment of being chained to a rock, subject to the perpetual torture of having his liver eaten away daily by an eagle.

In his poem and political-socialist allegory,

THE MYTH OF PROMETHEUS

"The Modern Prometheus" is the novel's subtitle. What does it mean?

In classical Greek legend, Prometheus was the Titan fire-God who stole fire from the Gods to give to mankind. Mary Shelley, Percy Bysshe Shelley and Lord Byron had all read the ancient Greek tragedy, *Prometheus Bound* by Aeschylus, and Byron wrote his own *Prometheus* in the same year Mary was writing *Frankenstein* (1816). But it was

Percy Shelley who assimilated the Promethean myth most completely to his poetic and socialist aspirations. In his political allegory, *Prometheus Unbound* (1919), Prometheus is presented as the heroic champion of mankind, defying divine tyranny and oppression, from impulses pure and just.

Percy Shelley's poem was a rehabilitation of a figure who, for the ancients, had been more reprehensible than heroic. His brilliant and bold theft of fire not only brought eternal punishment upon himself – the perpetual torture of being chained to a rock, an eagle eating away at his liver: it had also, in most versions of the myth, brought disaster upon mankind. The ambivalence of

Prometheus Unbound (1919), Shelley was to cast Prometheus as the hero of moral perfection and true motive, benefactor and champion of mankind, defying divine tyranny and oppression to save the human race. In the same way, Walton and Frankenstein are determined that any success they enjoy should rebound to the benefit of humankind – a far more important motive than the "enticement" of riches. "You cannot contest," writes Walton to his sister, "the inestimable benefit which I shall confer on all mankind to the last generation, by

the fire-bringer's gift – as at once life giving and life-destroying – is encapsulated in the monster's narrative in *Frankenstein*:

> One day, when I was oppressed by cold, I found a fire which had been left by some wandering beggars, and was overcome with delight at the warmth I experienced from it. In my joy I thrust my hand into the live embers, but quickly drew it out again with a cry of pain. How strange, I thought, that the same cause should produce such opposite effects... When night came again I found, with pleasure, that the fire gave light as well as heat and that the discovery of this element was useful to me in my food. (11)

"The same cause" is indeed productive of "opposite" effects when the monster uses "combustibles" to burn the cottage of the de Lacey family which has been a whole human world to him until the moment he is rejected by its inhabitants *(15)*.

If Frankenstein is "The Modern Prometheus", is he saviour or sinner? A hero of exalted endeavour on behalf of human progress or a calamitous over-reacher? The novel is inconclusive on the matter. What the subtitle does is exploit the equivocal potential of the Promethean legend to

discovering a passage near the pole" (Letter 1). "I entered with the greatest diligence into the search [for] the elixir of life," says Victor. "Wealth was an inferior object, but what glory would attend the discovery if I could banish disease from the human frame and render man invulnerable to any but a violent death!" (2). As Victor's teacher, Professor Waldman, puts it: "The labours of men of genius, however erroneously directed, scarcely ever fail in ultimately turning to the solid advantage of mankind" (4).

---

render any definitive answer to these questions impossible.

Had the subtitle invoked the other classic tale of over-reaching which haunts the novel's pages, the "moral" of the story might have been more explicit. For Frankenstein's "search for the philosopher's stone and elixir of life" is a version of the transgressive aspirations to immortality which belong to the medieval tradition of Faust, whose everlasting life and boundless granting of his wishes are bought at the price of surrendering his soul to the devil: Frankenstein's God-like ambition that "a new species would bless him as its creator and source" hovers between (what Shelley called) the "best and noblest ends" of Prometheus and the sheer arrogance and egotism of a Faust.

But so ambiguous is Mary Shelley's subtitle, as the novelist (and biographer of Mary) Muriel Spark has pointed out, that we do not even know to which character it applies: "Though at first Frankenstein is the Prometheus, the vital fire-endowing protagonist, the Monster, as soon as he is created, takes on [a different aspect of] the role." The attributes of the Promethean hero are split between the protagonists, so that Frankenstein defies divine power by creating life, but his creature suffers at least part of the consequences and punishment. ∎

For such ambitions, Frankenstein's "reach" – as the 19th-century poet and inheritor of Romanticism, Robert Browning, put it – "must exceed his grasp", must go, that is, beyond his own natural purview. Thus "Life and death" appear to Victor "ideal bounds, which I should first break through, and pour a torrent of light into our dark world" (4). The alternative to such "excess" is a cautious drawing back from the unknown – "with how many things are we on the brink of becoming acquainted, if cowardice or carelessness did not restrain our enquiries" (4) – or, worse still, an acceptance of compromise and of the narrow and secondary results of lesser achievements. "I had contempt," says Frankenstein "for the uses of modern natural philosophy" which sought not the "immortality and power" for which the ancients aimed but, instead, "to limit itself to the annihilation of those visions... I was required to exchange chimeras of boundless grandeur for realities of little worth" (3).

For Robert Kiely, Frankenstein's endeavour, and his monstrous creation itself, in part represents the Romantic valuing of "a great catastrophe" over a "small success". "A destructive force," says Kiely, was for the Romantics "better than no force at all and the creation of a new menace better than a copy of a worn-out consolation".

Even the fact that the monster becomes a murderer and brings about the destruction of his master does not necessarily detract from the grandeur of Frankenstein's dreams. If he has not been able to create human life, he has been able to create a sublime facsimile... There is a strong hint that the fault is more nature's than his, that his godlike ambitions result in monstrosity... The grotesqueness of the result [of Frankenstein's attempt to manufacture a man], is another example of nature's failure to live up to man's expectations.

The Shelleys and other Romantics like Byron, says Kiely,

were fascinated by the correspondence between the terrifying and the magnificent, the proximity of ruinous and constructive forces at the highest

FRANKENSTEIN AND THE RIME OF THE ANCIENT MARINER (1798)

———————

One of the founding texts of the Romantic movement, *The Ancient Mariner* (1798) was an early influence in Mary Shelley's life. It is reported that, as a young child, she heard Coleridge read the poem when he paid a visit to her father.

It tells the story of a sailor, shipwrecked by a storm at the South Pole, and led to clear waters following the appearance of an albatross. Believing the latter to be a bird of ill omen, the mariner cruelly shoots it, after which the ship falls under a curse, the crew hang the albatross around the despised mariner's neck, and the ship encounters Death in a ghostly hulk. While the crew perishes, the mariner's punishment is to wander from

levels of experience. "Nothing should shake the truly great spirit which is not sufficiently mighty to destroy it," said Shelley ... The risk of calamity becomes the measure of all endeavour... The catastrophic abomination represented by Frankenstein's creature is not proof of its creator's folly, but an inverse indication of his potential greatness.

Kiely's "Romantic" reading is arguably borne out, when, even at the last, Frankenstein looks back on his endeavours more with nostalgic pleasure than with loathing: "Even now I cannot recollect without passion my reveries while the work was incomplete. I trod heaven in my thoughts, now exulting in my powers, now burning with the idea

---

land to land, recounting his cautionary tale of deep and lonely terror:

Like one that on a
        lonesome road
Doth walk in fear and
        dread,
And having once turned
        round walks on,
And turns no more his
        head;
Because he knows, a
        frightful fiend
Doth close behind him
        tread.

These lines – which Percy Shelley described as the most frightening he had ever read – are recalled by Victor Frankenstein the very moment he abandons, in the sickness of fear and horror, "the demoniacal corpse to which I had so miserably given life" (5). Like the Ancient Mariner – to whose "worn and woeful" example Walton also compares his own (parallel) situation as he journeys by boat to the north pole – Victor will find himself not only pursued by his own guilt, and forced to confront the

of their effects" (24). Frankenstein bitterly regrets the *consequences* of his endeavour, but not his *capacity* for it. When Walton's men are on the brink of returning their vessel to shore, it is Frankenstein – defeated and dying as a consequence of his ambition – who says:

> *"Did you not call this a glorious expedition? And wherefore was it glorious? Not because the way was smooth and placid as a southern sea, but because it was full of dangers and terror... You were hereafter to be hailed the benefactors of your species; your names adored as belonging to brave men who encountered death for honour and the benefit of mankind."* (24)

blank waste of his life amid the "everlasting ices" of the earth, but compelled to narrate his story of persecution and punishment as an example to others.

But what the *Ancient Mariner* most powerfully gave to Mary Shelley was a model of "the Wanderer", not just for Frankenstein and Walton but for the monster too. A figure of primal guilt and alienation, of essential loneliness, he is a creature abandoned by his creator, cut off from his own kind and from his once whole self. He is an outcast whose crime is matched only by his suffering. Persecuted, defeated, anomalous, he offers something like the pain of original sin.

In the amendments Mary Shelley made to the novel in 1831, she uses the *Ancient Mariner* to suggest that trangressive stories like hers are born of an unfathomable dimension which is itself beyond human comprehension. "There is something at work in my soul that I do not understand," she wrote in her Journal. ∎

In his dying words, even as Frankenstein urges Walton to "seek happiness in tranquility and avoid ambition", he adds involuntarily: "Yet why do I say this? I have myself been blasted in these hopes but another may succeed" (24). Walton says of Frankenstein at the outset that "he has a double existence... he may suffer misery and be overwhelmed by disappointments" but he "seems still to have the power of elevating his soul from earth" (Letter 4). Arguably, this Romantic disposition for inhabiting the material and spiritual at once allows Frankenstein heroically to transcend the defeat he suffers within his own person, in order to envision, at the end of his life, what is needed for the future of the species.

Moreover, precisely where "actual achievement falters", Kiely argues, "the guilty and disappointed spirit can sketch the dimensions of its unfulfilled intention by describing the magnitude of its torment". The tragic-heroic depth and grandeur of Frankenstein's suffering impresses from his very first introduction – "He must have been a noble creature in his better days," Walton writes, "being even now in wreck so attractive and amiable... He excites at once my admiration and my pity to an astonishing degree" (Letter 4) – to his final and fatal demise: "What a glorious creature he must have been in the days of his prosperity, when he is thus noble and Godlike in ruin! He seems to feel his own worth and the greatness of his fall" (24).

Frankenstein's expression of his lonely personal pain, his perpetual experience of punishment and loss, makes him a powerfully Romantic figure: "The wounded deer dragging its fainting limbs to some untrodden brake, there to gaze upon the arrow which had pierced it, and to die – was but a type of me" (9). Not for nothing is the central Romantic icon of isolation, guilt and despair, the Ancient Mariner, several times invoked in this book.

"It was the Promethean 'maker', 'artist', 'shaper' of men in scientist-hero guise that interested Mary Shelley," says Maurice Hindle in his introduction to the Penguin edition of the novel, arguing nonetheless that the author's interest in the Promethean myth goes beyond its Romantic connotations. "In using the Promethean motif for her novel, she had virtually declared herself to be dealing with a problem" – mankind's relationship to forces larger than itself – "which had an enormously long and deep provenance in the West." *Frankenstein*'s relationship to ancient mortal problems, as well as its criticism of the Romantic tradition in which it was produced, are in the end arguably as strong as its self-evident Romantic credentials.

Opposite: Boris Karloff in his iconic portrayal of Frankenstein's monster in James Whale's 1931 film adaptation

Is Victor Frankenstein a monster?

Unhappy man! Do you share my madness? Have you drunk also of the intoxicating draught? Hear me; let me reveal my tale, and you will dash the cup from your lips. (Letter 4)

You seek for knowledge and wisdom, as I once did; and I ardently hope that the gratification of your wishes may not be a serpent to sting you as mine has been. (Letter 4)

SCIENCE AND THE SHELLEYS

For the most part, *Frankenstein* eschews the supernatural. It confines itself to the possible if not the probable. Indeed, Frankenstein's fictional scientific career echoes Percy Shelley's actual fascination with science, including magnetism (Walton's specific interest) as well as electricity and chemistry – fields in which he was an avid experimenter at Eton and Oxford.

Frankenstein, says Anne Mellor, "is a thought-experiment based directly on the work of three scientists":

*From the chemist and first President of the Royal Society of Science, Humphry Davy – whose work Mary Shelley read in the year she began the novel and who was revered by Percy – she derived the idea of the chemist as a "creative" scholar whose duty is not only to "interrogate" the "most

Learn from me... how dangerous is the acquirement of knowledge and how much happier that man is who believes his native town to be the world, than he who aspires to be greater than his nature will allow. (4)

One complicating factor in trying to understand what the figure of Frankenstein means, morally or allegorically, is the fact that this Romantic 'hero' of noble ambition casts himself unambiguously at the opening of the novel, and really throughout his account, as a Faustian over-reacher – one with God-usurping aspirations toward divine creativity. "I [have] always been imbued with a fervent longing to penetrate the secrets of nature" (2); "Whence...

profound secrets of nature" but to "change", "modify" and "master" it.

*From the botanist-poet (also admired by Shelley) Erasmus Darwin, grandfather of Charles Darwin and the first pioneer of the theory of evolution through sexual selection, she gleaned the alternative scientific stance of observation of the processes of nature rather then interference in her laws.

*And from Italian scientist, Luigi Galvani and his disciples, who attempted to reanimate dead animals – and even a human corpse – using electrical impulses, she took the idea for the central experiment of *Frankenstein*.

Mary Shelley's scientific interest was by no means neutral, however, argues Mellor:

> Frankenstein shares with early modern science the assumption that nature is only matter, particles that can be rearranged at the will of the scientist. [Modern scientists] thus

did the principle of life proceed? It was a bold question and one which has ever been considered a mystery" (4); "What had been studied and desired of the wisest men since the creation of the world was now within my grasp... A new species would bless me as its creator and source" (4).

The archetypal seeker of forbidden knowledge, Frankenstein transgresses the boundaries between the human and the natural, on the one hand, and the human and the divine, on the other. His tale owes its existence to its potential power as a cautionary parable. "I had determined at one time that the memory of these evils should die with me, but you have won me to alter my determination," Frankenstein tells Walton. "When I reflect that

---

defy an earlier Renaissance world-view that perceived nature as a living organism, Dame Nature or Mother Earth, with whom humans were to live in a cooperative, mutually beneficial communion.

In this interpretation of the novel as a part-feminist, part-ecological attack on the egoism of male scientific thought, Frankenstein's experiment fails to succeed, says Mellor, "not merely because the creature turns on him, but also because 'Mother Nature' fights back",

destroying Victor's health, preventing him from engendering his own natural child on his wedding-night, and relentlessly pursuing him with the elemental power – the lightning flashes of the raging storm on the Alpine peaks – which this modern Prometheus had stolen from her.

"Ultimately, in *Frankenstein* ... the penalty for pursuing Nature to her hiding places is death." Thus, almost giddyingly, does an exclusively secular and scientific reading resonate with the novel's central "religious" story of the Fall. ∎

you are pursuing the same course, exposing yourself to the same dangers which have rendered me what I am, I imagine that you may deduce an apt moral from my tale" (Letter 4). The very pretext for the story being told is the prevention, thereby, of its repetition, not just because of the monstrous consequences of Frankenstein's over-reaching but because of the magnitude of his Fall.

The forbidden understanding which Frankenstein explicitly seeks is that of the alchemists: the secret of eternal life. "I entered with the greatest diligence into the search for the philosopher's stone and the elixir of life" (2). But the discourse of "penetrating" the "hidden laws" and "secrets of nature" applies to scientific endeavour in general: "It was the secrets of heaven and earth that I desired to learn... in its highest sense, the physical secrets of the world" (2). Moreover, Frankenstein's processes of enquiry and discovery are not actually those of Faustian alchemy but those (grotesquely enough) of empirical scientific study. "The dissecting room and the slaughter-house furnished many of my materials," Frankenstein recounts:

I pursued nature to her hiding-places. Who shall conceive the horrors of my secret toil as I dabbled among the unhallowed damps of the grave or tortured the living animal to animate the lifeless clay?... I collected bones from charnel-houses and disturbed, with profane fingers, the tremendous

secrets of the human frame. In a solitary chamber,
or rather cell, at the top of the house, and separated
from all the other apartments by a gallery and
staircase, I kept my workshop of filthy creation. (4)

As Andrew Griffin pointed out in the 1970s, while "the movies make of Victor's laboratory a brilliant pyrotechnical display, full of light and energy", in the novel, by contrast, "all is cold horror – 'unhallowed damps', 'lifeless clay', 'dissecting-room' and 'slaughter-house'". Moreover, the emphasis of the text at this juncture of the story is not only upon Frankenstein's own incredulous horror and guilty shame at the unnaturalness of his proceedings: "My limbs now tremble, and my eyes swim with the remembrance... my eyeballs were starting from my sockets in attending to the details of my employment... often did my human nature turn with loathing from my occupation" (4). More pronounced still is the alienation from human society – and from his own "human nature" – into which his macabre enquiry leads him, as he is borne onward "like a hurricane, in the first enthusiasm of success" (4):

A resistless and almost frantic impulse urged me
forward; I seemed to have lost all soul and sensation
but for this one pursuit. (4)

I pursued my undertaking with unremitting ardour.
My cheek had grown pale with study, and my person

had become emaciated with confinement. (4)

*My employment, loathesome in itself, [had] taken
an irresistible hold of my imagination... The great
object... swallowed up every habit of my nature.* (4)

Even when Frankenstein acknowledges, amid his
revulsion, the abiding vigour of his endeavour – "In
other studies you go as far as others have gone
before you, and there is nothing more to know; but
in a scientific pursuit there is continual food for
discovery and wonder" – the text betrays the
absolute exclusiveness not only of the work but of
its special rewards. "*None but those who have
experienced them* can conceive the enticements of
science" (4).

For many readers, the obsessive nature of
Frankenstein's goal, and the way it is pursued, are
evidence, as David Punter puts it, that criticism of
"the illusion of pure scientific enquiry", shorn of
any interest in society or morality, "is one of the
major arguments of the book". Anne Mellor agrees.
Frankenstein, she says, is cited so often in everyday
life precisely because it engages the ethical
dimension of scientific invention.

The condemners of genetically modified meats
and vegetables now refer to them as
"Frankenfoods", and the debates concerning the
morality of cloning or stem cell engineering
constantly invoke [*Frankenstein's*] cautionary

example. Nor is the monster-myth cited only in regard to the biological sciences; critics of nuclear, chemical, and biological weapons alike often make use of this monitory figure.

For Mary Poovey, however, Mary Shelley's target is not science alone, but the pursuit of knowledge and truth per se, especially as it is manifested in art and poetry. *Frankenstein* is its *female* author's attack, argues Poovey, on the egotism she associates with the *male* "artist's monstrous self-assertion".

> When the individual loses or leaves the regulating influence of a relationship with others, imaginative energy always threatens to turn back on itself, to "mark" all external objects as its own... If [imaginative activity] is aroused but is not controlled by human society, it will project itself onto the natural world, becoming voracious in its search for objects to conquer and consume.

This principle, Poovey goes on, constitutes the major dynamic of *Frankenstein*'s plot, where the ego's destructiveness is made literal in setting in motion the character of the monster.

> What [Frankenstein] really wants is not to serve others but to assert himself... his "benevolent" scheme actually acts out the imagination's essential and deadly self-devotion... In effect, animating the monster completes and liberates

Frankenstein's egotism, for his indescribable experiment gives explicit and autonomous form to his ambition and desires.

For Poovey, *Frankenstein* is not a celebration of Percy Shelley's emancipatory poetics and politics, as some argue, but an imaginative criticism of his self-serving poetic ambitions.

Critics who take this view see *Frankenstein* as at root an anti-Romantic text which repeatedly stresses a fatal kinship between human imaginative desire and violent destruction and death:

> *When I would account to myself for the birth of that passion which afterwards ruled my destiny, I find it arise, like a mountain river, from ignoble and almost forgotten sources; but, swelling as it proceeded, it became the torrent which, in its course, has swept away all my hopes and joys. (20)*

Essentially opposed to creative liberation, Frankenstein's passion is like a travesty of Romantic-poetic inspiration.

That passion is also, in its hidden or forgotten source, unmistakably sexual and, for feminist critics, misplaced. For feminists, Frankenstein's deepest sin is the act of creation *without a woman* – "the story of a man," as Barbara Johnson observes, "who usurps the female role by physically giving birth to a child". Anne Mellor makes the same point: "Victor's quest is precisely to usurp from nature the female power of biological reproduction, to become a male womb." Mary Poovey writes:

> Frankenstein's particular vision of immortality and the vanity that it embodies have profound social consequences, because Frankenstein would deny relationships (and women) any role in the conception of children and because he would reduce all domestic ties to those that centre on and feed his selfish desires.

Seen from this angle, the arguments about gender and science in the book blend powerfully with its appropriation of the myth of Christian creation. But there is no agreement on how we should interpret *Frankenstein*; on the contrary, possible readings collide as if to prevent any definite understanding of what it is *really* "about". In this respect, *Frankenstein* exploits a form peculiarly suited to the sceptical treatment of final truths. As Robert Hume has pointed out, its threefold structure enacts a series of quests which not only invalidate one another but where quest itself is parodied in a circular journey to nowhere.

In what ways is Frankenstein's "miserable monster" monstrous?

How can I describe my emotions at this catastrophe, or how delineate the wretch whom with such infinite pains and care I had endeavoured to form?... I saw the dull yellow eye of the creature open; it breathed hard, and a convulsive motion agitated its limbs... His yellow skin scarcely covered the work of muscles and arteries beneath [his] shriveled complexion and straight black lips... No mortal could support the horror of that countenance. A mummy again endued with animation could not be so hideous as [the] demoniacal corpse to which I had so miserably given life. (5)

It is this emphasis upon the physical horror of the "wretch" that will be most familiar to contemporary readers who come to the original work, as many do, from films which depict Frankenstein's creature as an alien, unsympathetic being. Such interpretations edit out what is central to the book – the embedded narrative in which the monster speaks movingly in his own person. "Perhaps the most extraordinary undocumented theft of the twentieth century cinema," says Esther Schor, is that of the creature's eloquent language, forcing him to speak through his body and through his actions. Since Universal Pictures's 1931 *Frankenstein* [directed by James Whale and starring Boris Karloff as the monster], the creature's virtual muteness has been an adjunct of Karloff's huge, lumbering, deep-browed, flat-topped monster, with conduction bolts protruding from his head.

Without the monster's personal voice and account of motivation, one is left with the de-personalised factual events of his story: violence, child murder, ugly revenge, sexual desire.

FRANKENSTEIN ON FILM

In modern times, the power of *Frankenstein* as a story and as a myth stems largely from film versions of the novel. There were more than a dozen of these in the first half of the century alone, the most famous of which, James Whale's 1931 film for Universal Pictures, starring Boris Karloff, left an indelible mark on what *Frankenstein* "means" today.

Aside from defining – in Karloff's rectangular face and bolted neck – the monster's visual iconography for successive generations, the film also "upends", as Paul O'Flinn puts it, Mary Shelley's meaning. Not only is the monster's own voice and extensive personal story excised: in addition, where Mary Shelley's monster *saves* a drowning child (16), in the film he *drowns* a child. "The novel makes him human," O'Flinn concludes, "while the film makes him subhuman", and this "twisted" version of

But in stressing the creature's monstrosity, films are actually exploiting an image that was central to the Gothic tradition itself, where representations of the "other", the taboo, the transgressive were the stock in trade. Gothic or (its descendant) fantasy literature, says Rosemary Jackson in *The Literature of Subversion,*

characteristically attempts to compensate for a lack resulting from cultural constraints: it is a literature of desire, which seeks that which is experienced as absence and loss...

The explicit sadism and the emphasis on the link

Frankenstein's monster has never really been rehabilitated. (A 2015 film, set in modern day Los Angeles and seen entirely from the perspective of the monster, still characterises him more as an innocent primitive than as a creature of human emotion and eloquent thought.)

The 1931 film, released during America's Great Depression, arguably served an ideological agenda – as a warning against insurrectionary mob violence. Similarly, the film which initiated the "Hammer Horror" productions of the 1950s and 1960s – *The Curse of Frankenstein,* released

in 1957, directed by Terence Fisher and starring Christopher Lee and Peter Cushing – has been seen as another exploitation of the myth for ideological purposes. The emphasis this time, however, is very different. In the 1957 film, Peter Cushing's Frankenstein is unambiguously the villain and "real monster" – a scientist to fear and hate – and this version of the novel, argues O'Flinn, directly coincided with "the development of atomic bomb and the nightmare possibility of universal destruction at the hands of a deranged individual". The fact that *The*

between violence and sexuality in successive films – from the famous *The Curse of Frankenstein* (directed by Terence Fisher in 1935, with Peter Cushing as Frankenstein) onwards – have reinforced and prolonged the reputation of Mary Shelley's work as transgressive myth.

But, for some readers, Frankenstein's creature incarnates political as much as sexual transgression, representing more an expression of collective social fear than a release of culturally forbidden desire. In this reading, *Frankenstein* created an embodiment of all that English bourgeois society repudiated – both the subversive political energies it suppressed at home and the 'foreignness' it

---

Curse of Frankenstein was one of the most commercially successful films in the history of British cinema is evidence, for O'Flinn, that "Frankenstein's monster is most urgently hailed at times of crisis" and "ransacked for the terms of articulate cultural hysteria".

But the *Frankenstein* films cannot be neatly categorised. James Whale's second Universal classic in the genre, *The Bride of Frankenstein* (1835) – telling the story of Frankenstein's creation of a mate for the monster – is more a comedy than a horror film, paving the way for a series of spoof versions of the story, the most famous of which is probably Mel Brooks's *Young Frankenstein* (1974). Whale's 1935 interest in the novel's (unrealised) female creature, meanwhile, was reprised in Kenneth Branagh's *Mary Shelley's Frankenstein* (1994), a film which explores the Oedipal dimensions of the text and, in its imagery, the story's concern with the trauma of birth.

Perhaps the films which are most faithful to the experimental spirit of the original, however, are those which are bolder in reinventing the myth, Ridley Scott's *Blade*

sought imperially to subdue or enslave elsewhere. For H. L. Malchow, for example,

> Shelley's portrayal of her monster drew upon contemporary attitudes towards non-whites, in particular on fears and hopes of the abolition of slavery in the West Indies, as well as on middle-class apprehension of a Luddite proletariat... [The monster] has been constructed out of a cultural tradition of the threatening "Other" – whether troll or giant, gypsy or Negro – and from the dark inner recesses of xenophobic fear and loathing.

Runner (1982), being the most famous example. *Blade Runner* transplants the *Frankenstein* myth into an era of genetic engineering: it exchanges an Alpine glacial landscape for the film noir setting of 2019 Los Angeles, yet produces a kindred atmosphere of wasteland abandonment. The city is chaotically over-populated but, thanks to technology, the wealthy now live in "off-world" suburbs, leaving urban poverty and decay behind them. The monster equivalents are biological "replicants" produced to be off-world slaves on space colonies. Four escape enslavement and return to earth to seek their maker. Pursued and eventually killed as aberrant monsters, they also convert, by their sheer humanity and suffering plight, the bounty hunter hero (played by Harrison Ford) set to catch them.

The film reflects what some critics see as the central *Frankenstein* anxiety for a modern audience. Thomas Frentz and Janice Rushing, for instance, talk of

> a process of increasing mechanization of the human and humanization

Part of the emotional appeal of the text, particularly in the 19th century, concludes Malchow, is that it "presented the Other as a rebellious and ungrateful child that owed its very existence to a white male patron". Something of this appeal was still there in the 20th century, argues Paul O'Flinn, in a seminal essay on film adaptations of the novel. In James Whale's 1931 *Frankenstein* – released in the depths of the American Depression and aimed at instilling in a mass audience the dangers of "mass activity in times of crisis" – the monster is furnished with a criminal madman's brain and his subsequent story is "violent, insurrectionary and systematically denigrated". "'Bashing the monster' is the only way

of the machine, a process moving toward an ultimate end in which the machine is god and the human is reduced either to slavery or obsolescence.

Others have drawn attention to how the climactic encounter in *Blade Runner*, where the chief replicant spares the life of his pursuer out of pity, and then dies himself, recover the elegiac tone of the original novel. "What the film achieves," says Timothy Morton, "derives from the ways it fully appreciates what really makes the novel *Frankenstein* disturbing. This is not the creature's difference from, but his *similarity* to human beings." It asks the question: when does a human being become a person? And two centuries after the original it raises ethical and metaphysical problems with a new urgency given the advances of modern science.

"*Frankenstein* has become a vital metaphor," says George Levine, "peculiarly appropriate to a culture dominated by a consumer technology, neurotically obsessed with 'getting in touch' with its authentic self and frightened at what it is discovering." ∎

Daniel Radcliffe as Igor and James McAvoy as Victor in Paul McGuigan's 2015 film,
Victor Frankenstein

that the malice and degeneracy he represents can be resolved." Subversion in this interpretation, says O'Flinn, "is labeled, literally [in the jar which contains the faulty brain], ABNORMAL".

Literary-historical readings of the novel show that the idea of the threatening "Other" central to *Frankenstein* was, in fact, very real at the time it was written – in the threat posed to the English social order by the French Revolution of 1789.

Since the ancients, says Chris Baldick, the image of physical deformity has been used to suggest what is wrong with 'the body politic'. "When political discord and rebellion appear this 'body' is said to be not just diseased, but misshapen, abortive, monstrous." In the era just before *Frankenstein* was written, however, this imagery came with particular ferocity from the pens of those who opposed the age's revolutionary impetus. In Edmund Burke's *Reflections on the Revolution in France* (1790), the insurgent Parisian army is a pernicious and incoherent "monster" that "can hardly fail to terminate its movements in some great national calamity". The French revolution stalks forth exactly like an animated corpse.

> Vice assumes a new body... It is renovated in its new organs with fresh vigour... It walks abroad; it continues its ravages; whilst you are gibbetting the carcass, or demolishing the tomb.

For Burke, says Baldick, "the monster image" is a powerful means of understanding "the chaotic and

---

POLITICS AND *FRANKENSTEIN*

Mary Shelley, as her journal shows, was deeply interested in the French revolution of 1789. She not only read and re-read her parents' revolutionary writings alongside the work of Thomas Paine (*The Rights of Man*) and Jean-Jacques Rousseau, but also the work of the conservative anti-Jacobins, including Edmund Burke, ideological arch-enemy of her father.

Moreover, she witnessed the devastation wrought by Napoleon's military campaigns after the revolution as the memoir of her elopement with Percy in 1814 (Six Weeks Tour) makes clear. On the couple's second European trip, they travelled to Geneva, birthplace

confused nature of revolutionary events".

Burke's treatise, moreover, was an attack not only upon the revolutionaries in Europe but on their counterparts in England, the intellectual leader of whom at the time was Mary Shelley's father, William Godwin. His *Enquiry Concerning the Principles of Political Justice* (1793), in which he set out his principles for a new utopian world order (and in which he himself employs monstrous imagery to highlight the consequences of social injustice), was demonised by Burkean conservatives as the "spawn of the monster".

Mary Shelley dedicated her novel to her father, and for some readers *Frankenstein* is a powerful homage to her father's politics. She opposes his adversaries, in this view, by highlighting the social origins of monstrous deeds. Lee Sterrenburg,

of Jean-Jacques Rousseau (1712–1778) whose writings had helped to inspire the French Revolution of 1789.

Frankenstein's attitude to the revolution, as to so much else, is equivocal. The birthplace of Frankenstein's monster – Ingolstadt – was also the intellectual birthplace of the French revolution. On the other hand Mary Shelley, like her parents, admired Rousseau though her admiration, like her mother's, was by no means uncritical. Mary Wollstonecraft's feminist treatise *A Vindication of the Rights of Woman* is in part an attack on Rousseau's *Émile, or Treatise on Education,* the final part of which (concerned with Émile's female counterpart and wife-to-be, Sophie) suggests, says Wollstonecraft critically, that "the whole tendency of female education ought to be directed to one point: – to render them [women] pleasing". ■

however, has argued, in his influential critique of the novel, "Politics and Psyche in *Frankenstein*", that Mary Shelley's monstrous fiction is *not* an expression of filial loyalty, but an implicit critique of her father's rational republican views. For Sterrenburg, the monster imagery of *Frankenstein* is the beginning of Mary Shelley's repudiation of her radical birthright, a repudiation she later made clear.

> Since I lost Shelley [her husband, who died in 1822] I have no wish to ally myself to the Radicals – they are full of repulsion to me. Violent without any sense of justice – selfish in the extreme – talking without knowledge – rude, envious, & insolent – I wish to have nothing to do with them.

Pamela Clemit also sees the novel as a critique of revolutionary idealism. "Mary Shelley travesties radicalism's Utopian expectations on a grand scale. Victor Frankenstein aspires to a 'new species', but ends up fearing a 'race of devils', and his fantasy of benefiting mankind is replaced by the apocalyptic dread of inflicting a 'curse upon everlasting generations' and wiping out 'the whole human race'."

But this is not to argue that the novel is a straightforward attack on revolutionary politics. Mary Shelley's monster is "a hybrid", argues Lee Sterrenburg:

> a cross between two visions that produces a

unique third. From the Burkean tradition of horrific, evil, and revolutionary monsters, he seems to have derived the grotesque features which physically mark him and set him apart. From the republican tradition he derives his rationale for insurrection. But Mary Shelley does more than conflate the two traditions. She moves inside the mind of the monster and asks what it is like to be labeled, defined and even physically distorted by a political stereotype. This is a new perspective. It is something her Enlightenment forerunners could not see, preoccupied as they were with charting, explaining and debating the external influences which enkindle revolution.

Frankenstein's monstrous creation should be seen not merely as a reaction against the Utopianism of Godwin, nor against the conservatism of Burke, says Sterrenburg, but rather as a response to the entire world-view of the Enlightenment-revolutionary age, with its omission of the personal for the sake of the social. "Mary Shelley exploits the first-person narrative as a means of internalizing public issues, moving away from the direct public engagement of the 1790s" to explore the psychology of political radicalism.

TEN FACTS ABOUT
FRANKENSTEIN

1.

When *Frankenstein* first appeared anonymously in 1818, it was an immediate bestseller, though it provoked mostly hostile reviews. The vitriol was provoked by the fact that *Frankenstein*'s first readers assumed, from its dedication to Mary Shelley's father, that the novel had been written by William Godwin, or by the author's husband, Percy Shelley, Godwin's best-known acolyte. The novel's dedication offered an opportunity for denunciation of the whole Godwin circle.

2.

It is true, however, that Percy Shelley revised his wife's content quite extensively – with her consent.

3.

In the Villa Diodati by Lake Geneva where she started writing *Frankenstein*, wine flowed copiously, according to Tom Perrottet in *The New York Times*, as did laudanum, a form of liquefied opium. "One night, when Byron read aloud a haunting poem, Shelley leapt up and ran shrieking from the room, having hallucinated that Mary had sprouted demonic eyes in place of nipples. It was in this surreal, claustrophobic atmosphere that she experienced the famous nightmare that became the lurid plot of *Frankenstein*."

4.
Mary Shelley said she made up the name "Frankenstein". But it is a German word which means Stone of the Franks. In fact, according to the historian Radu Floresci, the Shelleys visited Castle Frankenstein on a journey up the Rhine and may have heard, while there, about an unbalanced alchemist, Konrad Dippel, who once lived in the castle. He was trying to create an elixir – Dippel's Oil – which would enable people to live for more than 100 years. Like Victor Frankenstein, Dippel was rumoured to dig up graves and experiment on dead bodies.

5.
The year Mary wrote *Frankenstein* came to be known as "the year without a summer". The eruption, in April the year before, of Mount Tamboro in Indonesia, sent clouds of volcanic ash into the upper atmosphere and caused, in effect, a long volcanic winter. The discovery by scientists of large dark spots on the sun added to the general sense of unease and impending doom – a sense reflected in Lord Byron's apocalyptic poem *Darkness*, and, of course, in *Frankenstein*.

6.

Frankenstein was not the only novel to emerge from the conclave at the Villa Diodati that miserable summer. John Polidori's novel *The Vampyre* – original of the vampire genre in fiction – also originated there, inspired by a short, fragmentary tale by Byron. Polidori was Byron's doctor.

7.

Brian Aldiss has argued that *Frankenstein* should be considered the first true science fiction story because, in contrast to previous stories with fantastical elements resembling those of later science fiction, the central character "makes a deliberate decision" and "turns to modern experiments in the laboratory" to achieve fantastic results.

8.

Mary added her own Preface, explaining the genesis of the work, to the 1831 edition, where she also made major revisions to her story. Some critics think the later version of the work, by a more mature Mary Shelley, 'tames' the revolutionary energies and vision of the youthful original, emphasizing conservative values as opposed to subversive ones. Elizabeth, for example, who is Victor's cousin in the original, becomes an adopted foundling, not directly related to him as in the 1831 version, thus rendering the couple's quasi-incestuous relationship more conformist.

9.

Frankenstein's cultural legacy in other media and popular culture seems boundless. Its influence is palpable from the TV show *The Addams Family* (1964-6) to the hit comic horror musical *The Rocky Horror Show* (first performed in 1973); from the 1970s Marvel Comics, *The Frankenstein Monster*, to contemporary interactive multi-media games; from the pop hit 'Monster Mash' (1963) to the heavy metal music of Black Sabbath into the 1990s; from adult erotica to techno-thrillers and dystopias, *The Terminator* (1984), *Robocop* (1987), *AI* (2001).

10.

It has been suggested that Mary Shelley may have taken Frankenstein's Christian name, Victor, from *Paradise Lost*. Milton often refers to God as the Victor, while Shelley sees Frankenstein as playing God by creating life.

In what ways is the monster Frankenstein's double?

Could he be the murderer... of my brother? No sooner did that idea cross my imagination than I became convinced of its truth... I considered the being whom I had cast among mankind and endowed with the will and power to effect purposes of horror... nearly in the light of my own vampire, my own spirit let loose from the grave and forced to destroy all that was dear to me. (7)

I, the true murderer, felt the never-dying worm alive in my bosom, which allowed of no hope or consolation. (8)

Incorporated in the idea of the "double" are all those unfulfilled but possible futures to which we still like to cling in fantasy, all those strivings of the ego which adverse circumstances have crushed, and all our suppressed acts of volition which nourish in us the illusion of Free Will. (Sigmund Freud, "The Uncanny", 1919)

What should we make of the murder – by the monster – of Victor's younger brother, William? Psychoanalytic critics see it, and the schizophrenic language which it produces in Victor – "I, not in deed, but in effect, was the true murderer" (9) – as an expression of the creator-hero's own suppressed fraternal hostility and rivalry. "In an orgy of narcissism, and as a sort of horrible retribution," writes Lowry Nelson, Frankenstein has succeeded in creating his own 'Doppelgänger', or 'double'.

The monster, in this reading, is a nightmare projection of Victor's unconscious urges, the embodiment of his primitive being which has been rejected, expelled, split away and located in another, in order to enact the monstrous, repressed desires which the civilised, controlling Ego dare not acknowledge. "The monster has no name," says Rosemary Jackson. "It is anonymous, given identity only as Frankenstein's other, his grotesque reflection (hence the common confusion of the monster *as* Frankenstein)." It is altogether appropriate, psychologically, that the monster has been popularly christened with the name of its creator. For, on this psychoanalytic reading, its murderous impulses are not in rebellion against his creator. ("You are my creator, but I am your master," says the monster (20).) Rather, its actions are working to fulfill its originator's deepest impulses. The monster is not supernatural, as Lowry puts it, but *sub*natural – the "irrational, the impulse to evil, the uncontrollable unconscious".

As George Levine points out, the psychoanalytic resonances of this book are unavoidable given that

all the battery of Freudian equipment comes

explosively into play – moral isolation, the grubbing in filthy flesh, the obsessed and inhuman energies which went into the creation of the monster, and the confrontation with the buried self which the monster's destructiveness really implies.

The first clear sign that we are witnessing the drama of a pre-Freudian psychology occurs at the moment the monster first comes to life. "Unable to endure the aspect of the being I had created," Victor relates, "I rushed out of the room... and threw myself on the bed":

> *I slept... but I was disturbed by the wildest dreams. I thought I saw Elizabeth, in the bloom of health, walking in the streets of Ingolstadt. Delighted and surprised, I embraced her, but as I imprinted the first kiss on her lips, they became livid with the hue of death; her features appeared to change and I thought that I held the corpse of my dead mother in my arms; a shroud enveloped her form, and I saw the grave-worms crawling in the folds of the flannel. I started from my sleep with horror; a cold dew covered my forehead, my teeth chattered, and every limb became convulsed.* (5)

The instantaneous revenge which the monster exacts is a psychic one, in which the hero is forced to confront the regressive depths of his being in an oedipal-necrophilic* nightmare which is doubly incestuous (he kisses first his dead cousin, virtually his sister, and thence his dead mother). The image of the mother resurfaces in the context of death and guilt when Justine, another family figure, is found with the locket bearing the picture of Victor's mother, which William had worn, and which has been planted on Justine by the monster. When Justine is then convicted of and executed for the boy's murder, "This also was my doing!" is Victor's instant confession to himself.

The submerged sibling and oedipal fantasies take place, moreover, within a fantastical narrative where the forbidden knowledge of which Victor is in pursuit is both explicitly sexual – he seeks the key to human reproduction – and repeatedly expressed in a "phallic" language: his goal is to "penetrate" what is 'secret" and "hidden", primal and dangerous. As Mary Jacobus says of what she calls Frankenstein's "postpartum nightmare":

> the composite image, mingling eroticism and the horror of corruption... the grave as well as the source of life, [brings] birth, sex and death together in one appalling place, the incestuously embraced mother [suggesting] Frankenstein's unnatural pursuit of nature's secrets in his

* oedipal as in the Oedipus Complex, Freud's theory that all young boys at a deep subsconscious level want to marry their mothers and kill their fathers; necrophilic from necrophilia, meaning sexual attraction to or intercourse with corpses.

charnel house labours.

Moreover, the dream is prophetic. The monster's repeated fiendish threat to Frankenstein, when the latter refuses to provide him with a mate – "Remember, *I will be with you on your wedding-night*" – is brutally fulfilled in the murder of Elizabeth before her marriage to Victor is consummated. Assuming himself to be the object of the monster's avenging rage, and "reflecting how fearful the combat I momentarily expected would be to my wife" (23), he entreats her to retire and virtually condemns her to her death.

She was there, lifeless and inanimate, thrown across the bed, her head hanging down and her pale and distorted features half covered by her hair... her bloodless arms and relaxed form flung by the murderer on its bridal bier... I rushed towards her and embraced her with ardour, but the deadly languor and coldness of the limbs told me that what I now held in my arms had ceased to be the Elizabeth whom I had loved and cherished. (23)

The monster's vanquishing of the bride has been interpreted, variously, as expressive of Frankenstein's neurotic fear of sexual union; his renounced phallic self; his misogynistic horror of female sexuality; the withdrawal from physical and emotional contact which characterised his scientific labours; anxiety at the loss of self-sufficiency and independence; Frankenstein's solipsistic sexuality, and the narcissism of his every act.

To underline the psychic importance of the event, Frankenstein, hanging over Elizabeth's body, sees at the open window, as if by moonlit mirror-image, "a figure the most hideous and abhorred", jeering and grinning, "his fiendish finger pointed towards the corpse of my wife" (23). It is a macabre black-comic image of the vengeful return of repressed primal energies.

For some critics, the presence of these unconscious sexual elements is the very essence of Gothic and, as such, an emancipation for the reader as much as for the protagonist. Rosemary Jackson, for example, thinks that fantastic literature "attempts to create a space for a discourse other than a conscious one". It reveals "an obscure, occluded region which lies behind the homely and native".

The subversive element of the genre can also be seen as liberating, as Robert Miles suggests:

The Gothic novel works as a dream of oppression from which one happily wakes up... [It offers] powerless citizens living under despotism an alternative interior realm in which to exercise power – over themselves: the experience of fulfillment in self-fulfilment. Gothic fiction [provided a realm] in which the politically disinherited could secure a self-fulfilment otherwise unavailable to them.

But some of the most influential readings of *Frankenstein*, especially feminist ones, find a psychology specific to its hero. The particular nature of his own self-fulfilment – eschewing natural procreation in order to bring a corpse to life – is, as Mary Jacobus puts it, an "exclusion of woman from creation" which symbolically "kills" the mother. Mary Homans makes much the same point. "The demon's birth," she says,

> violates the normal relations of family, especially the normal sexual relation of husband and wife. Victor has gone to great lengths to produce a child without Elizabeth's assistance... To circumvent her, to make her unnecessary, is to kill her and to kill mothers altogether.

This psychic killing occurs within a plot, as Homans points out, in which mother-death abounds. Elizabeth, Justine, and Frankenstein's own mother are as orphaned in this respect as is the monster. Moreover, the monster not only depends upon but perpetuates the death of the mother and of motherhood when, in killing Elizabeth, he murders "the last remaining potential mother". For Homans, this wholesale "circumvention of the maternal" is of a piece with Mary Shelley's implicit criticism of the male Romantic artistic ego: "The new creation of the demon in the image of the self [is a substitute] for the powerful creating mother and places creation under the control of the son."

Even as the novel's doublings and displacements seem to summon psychic and symbolic interpretation, they contribute nonetheless to the gripping narrative of persecution and pursuit which occupies the final third of the novel. "As a recognizable human world recedes and the Creature becomes a progressively more enthralling superpower," says Paul Sherwin in his influential essay, '*Frankenstein*: Creation as Catastrophe', "Frankenstein, now wholly the creature's creature, joins in the frenetic dance of death that impels these mutually fascinated antagonists across the waste places of the earth".*

But, for Sherwin, the "astonishing achievement of *Frankenstein*" is the construction of a primal, erotic and catastrophically total repression "so radically alienated from the ego that it disqualifies any attempt at integration". The monster, in other words, is not reducible to interpretation as Frankenstein's alter ego or to any psychoanalytic interpretation. For what it represents is Chaos itself, the unformed and uncontrolled *within*. Frankenstein calls the unnameable creature "my own spirit let loose from the grave... forced to destroy all that was dear to me" (7).

Sherwin's psychoanalytic reading of the

---

* This "symbiotic unit" is also located, argues Bernard Duyfhuizen, in an identity of language – the term "wretch" applying to both creature and creator and never far from a term of endearment," Periphrastic Naming in Mary Shelley's *Frankenstein*", *Studies in the Novel* (1995).

monster's meaning recalls the monster's association with the political anarchy threatened by
revolution. It is also barely separable from the idea
of Hell which the novel borrows from *Paradise
Lost*.

In what ways is Frankenstein's monster virtuous?

What gives special power to the monster's story is
its "inhuman" capacity to do what no mere mortal
narrative could do. The story begins, that is to say,
at the *very* beginning:

> *I was a poor, helpless, miserable wretch; I knew, and
> could distinguish, nothing; but feeling pain invade
> me on all sides, I sat down and wept.* (11)

> *No distinct ideas occupied my mind; all was
> confused. I felt light, and thunder and thirst and
> darkness; innumerable sounds rang in my ears, and
> on all sides various scents saluted me.* (11)

The monster's creation may be artificial, but – from
the monster's point of view – the moment and
trauma of his birth is an experience entirely human.
He is first bathed in the created world, a repository

of innocent sensory responsiveness to its formless wonder: "soon a gentle light stole over the heavens and gave me a sensation of pleasure. I started up and beheld a radiant form rise from among the trees" (11). Thence he undergoes the familiar human stages of growth and adaptation – "distinguishing sensations from each other" and perceiving the boundaries and forms of things, "the radiant roof of light which canopied me... the clear stream that supplied me with drink... the pleasant sound... from the throats of the little winged animals" (11). In this accelerated version of both infant and species development, he also discovers involuntarily his need to communicate: "Sometimes I tried to imitate the pleasant songs of the birds... but the uncouth and inarticulate sounds which broke from me frightened me into silence again" (11).

Frankenstein's monster begins life as the kind of "natural man" imagined by Jean-Jacques Rousseau – the "noble savage" whose primitive instinct for life "know[s] neither hatred nor revenge". On the contrary, this pre-civilised creature possesses an innate responsiveness to goodness and love. When he occupies the hovel next to the de Lacey family and observes their daily life, their benevolence and gentleness win his reverence:

The young girl... sat down beside the old man, who, taking up an instrument, began to play and to produce sounds sweeter than the voice of the thrush or the nightingale. It was a lovely sight, even to me, poor wretch! who had never beheld aught beautiful before. (11)

The monster's original goodness is the source of his sentiment – "when they were unhappy, I felt depressed; when they rejoiced I sympathized in their joys" (12) – as it is the spring of his action. When he finds that his nightly habit of stealing food for his own sustenance is inflicting pain upon the family (who are also hungry), he uses the night-time to collect firewood for them instead.

What the monster really offers in his "infant" stages is an animated illustration of William Godwin's theory of human perfectibility: born innocent – a *tabula rasa*, or blank sheet, susceptible to the circumstances in which he is placed – he is formed in relation to the good influences which act upon him. "I looked upon crime as a distant evil: benevolence and generosity were ever-present before me" (15).

As natural man, altruistically taking creation as he finds it, the monster seems, moreover, not his creator's double but his antithesis – he does not share Frankenstein's egoistic will or desire to conquer nature's secrets. As an educated being, his learning confirms and extends his instinctive morality and sense of human relations instead of providing, as was the case with Frankenstein, the means to usurp them. Goethe's *The Sorrows of Werther* impresses the monster with its "lofty sentiments and feelings, which had for their object, something out of self" (15); reading the political history, *Plutarch's Lives,* he feels "the greatest ardour for virtue rise within me, and abhorrence for vice" (15).

But when the monster's virtue cannot survive contact with the human society he craves, his story offers an object lesson in Rousseau's and Godwin's belief in the corrupting power of civilisation. In return for his instinctive species-love and his longing to "join them", humans repay the creature's near approach with fear and horror, flight and disgust. Not even the enlightened de Laceys, whom the creature has looked upon as "superior beings who would be the arbiters of my future destiny" (12), can overcome the universal hostility and overlook his deformity: "a fatal prejudice clouds their eyes, and where they ought to see a feeling and kind friend, they behold only a detestable monster" (15). With no knowledge of his origin or parentage, the monster has no other judge or measure of his own intrinsic worth:

> *I had admired the perfect forms of my cottagers – their grace, beauty and delicate complexions: but how was I terrified when I viewed myself in a transparent pool... I became convinced that I was indeed the monster that I am.* (12)

It was an axiom of Godwinian political theory that monsters are not born; they are made. Evil is not inherent but imposed by the inequalities and oppressions of corrupt institutions. As Percy Shelley put it, in his review of *Frankenstein* (posthumously published in *The Athenaeum* in 1832):

> Treat a person ill and he will become wicked...
> divide him, a social being from society, and you
> impose upon him the irresistible obligations
> – malevolence and selfishness.

"I, the miserable and the abandoned," the creature says to Walton at the close of the novel, "am an abortion, to be spurned at, and kicked, and trampled on. Even now my blood boils at the recollection of this injustice" (24). Unloved and alone – abused, abandoned, ill-treated – the creature becomes monstrous indeed:

> *My feelings were those of rage and revenge... There*
> *was none among the myriads of men that existed*
> *who would pity or assist me; and should I feel*
> *kindness toward my enemies? No; from that moment*
> *I declared ever-lasting war against the species.* (16)

Just so, the violent energies of insurrection are unleashed by arbitrary social injustice. This is why, for many readers, the creature offers a sympathetic embodiment of the forces and needs which motivated the terror of the French revolution. If, at one level, the creature's perversion is an image of the psychological damage that flows from social oppression and tyranny, at another level, his physical

Helena Bonham Carter and Kenneth Branagh in the 1994 film Mary Shelley's
Frankenstein

deformity is itself an analogue of the institutional-
ised distortions of social injustice itself.

> *I learned that the possession most esteemed by your
> fellow creatures were high and unsullied descent
> united with riches. A man without either [was
> considered] a vagabond and a slave... And what was
> I? I possessed no money, no friends, no kind of
> property... Was I, then, a monster, a blot upon the
> earth?* (13)

"It is precisely the creature's anomalous status that
makes him so terrifying to the human others who
encounter him," says Graham Allen in his
Godwinian reading of the novel:

But that terror is founded on the possibility that the creature's anomalous nature might *reflect* the human rather than simply differing from it [my emphasis]... The creature is such a threat to human society because he is a visible sign and reminder of the abortive nature of humanity itself.

The monster is not only Frankenstein's double, but *our own*. In this reading, the monster is only the grossest example of the perversions of natural justice and humanity which injure almost every individual or social grouping in the book – from the wrongly condemned Justine, to the de Lacey family and Safie's father, who suffer at the hands of governmental authorities which abuse their powers.

Moreover, when the novel is read as a political parable, it is not the monster who is at fault, but his creator:

Where were my friends and relations? [those which] bind one human being to another in mutual bonds. No father had watched my infant days, no mother had blessed me with smiles and caresses... All my past life was now a blot, a blind vacancy... Of my creation and creator I was absolutely ignorant. (13)

Ironically, Frankenstein had boasted at the start of his enterprise: "Many happy and excellent natures would owe their being to me. No father could claim the gratitude of his child so completely as I should deserve theirs" (4). But, arguably, Frankenstein's chief error is not that of Romantic or scientific-intellectual hubris: it is a paternal one. His great mistake is not creating the monster, but refusing to take responsibility for it. His first act in relation to his creature is to disown it. When they meet again face to face on Mont Blanc, and the monster asks for love from his creator, the latter hurls execrations at him ("Begone, vile insect!... Abhorred monster! Fiend that thou art!... Wretched devil!"), sealing a vicious circle of rejection and revenge, which the monster describes with penetrating and persuasive accuracy. "I am malicious because I am miserable" (17). "I was benevolent and good; misery made me a fiend. Make me happy, and I shall again be virtuous" (10).

When Frankenstein abandons his creature, he offers at once an allegory of the neglect of a parent and a warning of the abominations which can result from this neglect. "Frankenstein's negligence leaves the creature no option but to repeat his own tyrannical actions," says Pamela Clemit.

What is more, the creature knows this. His insistence upon the primary value of familial and communal human relations is deeply rational, a model of Godwinian polemic.

My vices are the children of a forced solitude that I abhor, and my virtues will necessarily arise when I live in communion with an equal. I shall feel the affections of a sensitive being and become linked to the chain of existence and events from which I am now excluded. (17)

There is no better measure of the creature's keen and exemplary power of reason than the fact that Frankenstein, detesting the idea of a second creature with all the revulsion he feels for the first, is himself convinced by the monster's case that he should be provided with a companion: "I was moved. I shuddered when I thought of the possible consequences... but I felt that there was some justice in his argument" (17).

But for all the strong Godwinian heritage which animates the monster, he is also consistently expressive – especially in this insistence on having a mate – of a world view that is Mary Shelley's own: the belief, as she writes in her own essay on Rousseau, that "the most characteristic part of man's nature is his affections".

"Affection", not reason: this, it seems, is the basis of human perfectibility for Mary Shelley. It is what Walton and Frankenstein both have as a birthright and what, for the sake of adventurism, they both eschew even as they feel acutely the sacrifice: "I bitterly feel the want of a friend," is Walton's lament at the very outset of the book (Letter 2). Frankenstein once enjoyed the "living spirit of love" (2), engendered by the company of Elizabeth and Clerval in his childhood, and his mournful regret at how this was exchanged for the "gloomy and narrow reflections upon self" (2) is given priority as his own story begins. For Robert Kiely "the most explicit 'moral' theme of the novel" is that "man discovers and fulfills himself through others and destroys himself alone". The counter-theme to the monstrous consequences of egotism "is the virtue of friendship".

Of the three protagonists, however, it is the monster – he alone who is denied a friend – who speaks most powerfully of love as an existential necessity. Witnessing, from his hovel, the kindness and affection of the de Lacey family, the monster experiences

> *sensations of a peculiar and over-powering nature; they were a mixture of pain and pleasure, such as I had never before experienced, either from hunger or cold, warmth or food; and I withdrew from the window, unable to bear these emotions* (11).

This is the pain of love needed and not received; it is also the pain of love ungiven. It is not the creature's monstrosity alone which speaks of the damage of being excluded from love, nor even the powerful reason with which he outsmarts and convinces Frankenstein. It is the evidence of his own plaintively eloquent voice: "Everywhere I see bliss, from which I alone am irrevocably excluded"; "I have no relation or friend upon the earth".

Is the monster the novel's hero?

Amid all the extraordinary reversals in this novel, perhaps the most startling is the way the monster becomes... the intellectual and moral superior of his creator. (George Levine)

Surprisingly, it is not by way of the priggish and "self-devoted" young scientist that Mary Shelley discovers the great power of her narrative but by way of the misshapen demon, with whom most

FRANKENSTEIN AND PARADISE LOST

Mary Shelley was brought up in a family circle where John Milton's *Paradise Lost* was required reading. Mary Shelley re-read the poem twice in 1815 and 1816; lines from *Paradise Lost* provide the epigraph to *Frankenstein;* the monster himself reads the work in Chapter 15.

The epic telling of the Biblical story of the Fall of Man, the poem recounts the temptation of Adam and Eve by the fallen archangel, Satan, and their subsequent casting out from the Garden of Eden.

The narrative begins in Hell, to which Satan and his fellow angels have been banished following their failed attempt to usurp God's authority. There, they plan to exact revenge for their ejection from Heaven by leading God's new creation, Man, to disobedience against God's law: Adam and Eve have been commanded, on punishment of death, not to eat from the tree of the knowledge of good and evil. When Satan, disguised as a serpent, persuades Eve to eat

readers identify. He has the most compelling speeches in the novel and is far wiser and more magnanimous than his creator. (Joyce Carol Oates)

Though it tends to be ignored by film-makers... the drastic shift in point of view that the nameless monster's monologue represents probably constitutes *Frankenstein's* most striking technical *tour de force,* just as the monster's bitter self-revelations are Mary Shelley's most impressive and original achievement. (Sandra Gilbert and Susan Gubar)

the fruit, Adam, finding that Eve has transgressed and is lost, eats the fruit too, in order to share the sin. At the close of the poem, they leave Paradise together, in some of the most haunting lines of Western literature:

> The world was all before
>   them, where to choose
> Their place of rest, and
>   Providence their guide:
> They, hand in hand, with
>   wandering steps and slow,
> Through Eden took their
>   solitary way.

What, above all, made *Paradise Lost* a potent work for the Romantics, and especially for those in Mary Shelley's immediate group, was the tragic-heroic depiction of Satan, whose refusal to be subjugated appealed strongly to the Romantics. When the monster understands *Paradise Lost* as the story "of an omnipotent God warring with his creatures", he echoes Mary Shelley's father William Godwin's own interpretation of Satan's rebellion as an illustration of the dangers of paternalistic tyranny. Percy Shelley felt the same way, arguing in *A Defense of Poetry* (1821) that "Milton's Devil as a moral being" is "far superior to his God". ∎

One reason the monster's narrative is, for some, one of the most moving in literature is that the monster, more than any other character, thoroughly embodies the novel's central myth. Right at the heart of this book – at its deep centre, literally, in this work of stories-within-stories – is the monster's own version of the Christian myth of the Fall.

The myth is mediated for the novel's protagonist, as it was for its author, by John Milton's 17th-century epic poem, *Paradise Lost*, virtually the bible itself for Mary Shelley and her Romantic circle. Adam's famous heavy lament, in Book 10 of *Paradise Lost*, as he realises his fallen condition ("the end/Of this new glorious world, and me so late/The Glory of that Glory... whom Death must end") provides the epigraph to Mary Shelley's novel:

> Did I request thee, Maker, from my clay
> To mould me man? Did I solicit thee
> From darkness to promote me?

When the monster himself reads *Paradise Lost* in Chapter 15, it is this picture of a creature who has no say in his own creation, and yet suffers most of all for the consequences of it, which stirs "far deeper emotions" than the monster has ever known before. "I read it," he says "as a true history... I often referred the several situations to my own." These are also the novel's explicit internal directions to the reader to recognise how the monster's story parallels and reproduces the grand religious narrative of Western civilisation, the myth of origins, and especially those aspects of the myth which were most potent for Romanticism.

The first striking echo of Adam's situation is the monster's experience of knowledge as inevitable suffering.

Sorrow only increased with knowledge. Oh, that I had forever remained in my native wood, nor known nor felt beyond the sensations of hunger, thirst, and heat!" (13)

Of what a strange nature is knowledge! It clings to the mind, when it has once seized on it, like a lichen on the rock. I wished sometimes to shake off all thought and feeling, but I learned there was but one means to overcome the sensation of pain, and that was death – a state which I feared yet did not understand. (13)

Increase of knowledge only discovered to me more clearly what a wretched outcast I was. (15)

Knowledge for the monster is what it was in the Garden of Eden – the consciousness of good and evil. That same knowledge of the deepest truth of things which was the prized goal for Victor Frankenstein, is, for his creature, the terrible condition of innocence lost – and lost forever – that it was for the first man. To the rebellious Romantic-Promethean urges of his hero-creator, the monster opposes the heroic-Romantic sensibility expressed painfully by Byron's guilt-ridden protagonist in *Manfred*, a Gothic verse-drama written in the same year as *Frankenstein* (1816):

> Sorrow is knowledge; they who know the most
> Must mourn the deepest o'er the fatal truth:
> The tree of knowledge is not life.

Not for nothing is the monster's plaintive cry – "And now, with the world before me, whither should I bend my steps?" – a direct echo of the poignant words of Adam and Eve as they leave the Garden of Eden. In the monster, Mary Shelley embodied the optimistic belief in original innocence which inspired Romantic politics, and the pain of expulsion from primordial innocence into a mortal hell of sin and death – the world of "the never-dying worm" (8) – which gave spiritual depth to the most rational and secular Romantic philosophies.

But the monster's strongest claims to status as the Romantic hero of the novel is his conscious likeness to Milton's demonised archangel, Satan: "I remembered Adam's supplication to his Creator... But where was mine?" "Many times I considered Satan as the fitter emblem of my condition," he says, "for often, like him" – who witnessed with mingled jealousy and admiration the paradisal state of Adam and Eve – "when I viewed the bliss of my protectors, the bitter gall of envy rose within me" (15). When the de Laceys spurn and desert him, a rage of anger at his unsympathised state impels him to "spread havoc and destruction around me, and...enjoy the ruin'; 'I, like the archfiend, bore a hell within me." Though "I ought to be thy Adam," he tells Frankenstein, "I am rather thy fallen angel" (10).

Satan's capacity to elicit awe, fear and terror deeply impressed the Romantic imagination, for which his purpose as intrepid avenger and devilish usurper of God's power was an equivocal virtue. As a Romantic reincarnation of the heroic fiend, the monster is all the more sympathetic for being undeservedly thrown from grace and being only reluctantly a serpent-devil. When, like Satan, he demolishes his former Eden – placing "a variety of combustibles around the cottage [I] destroyed every vestige of cultivation in the garden" (16) – he is even yet the would-be angel: "*Unable to injure anything human*, I turned my fury towards inanimate objects" (16).

And even when, thereafter, the monster unleashes his uncontrollable demonic rage upon the innocent child, William, and thence seizes the glacier for his domain as Milton's devil embraced the profoundest hell, he rises to the stature of his literary forebear, not only in his superhuman strength and size, but in the grandeur of his eloquence: "You, my creator, detest and spurn me... to whom thou art bound by ties only dissoluble by the annihilation of one of us. You purpose to kill me. How dare you sport thus with life?" (10)

"Nothing," wrote Percy Shelley, "can exceed the energy and magnificence of the character of Satan as expressed in *Paradise Lost.*" Mary Shelley's own creature of transgressive excess comes close, however, not least because of his constant capacity to mutate. Joyce Carol Oates writes:

> The inhuman creation becomes increasingly human while his creator becomes increasingly inhuman. Most suggestively, he has become by the novel's melodramatic conclusion a form of Christ: sinned against by all human kind, yet fundamentally blameless, and *yet* quite willing to die as a sacrifice: "soon... I shall die. Soon these burning miseries will be extinct." (24)

Yet, if the monster is a more sympathetic version of Milton's Satan, he is also far worse off than him: "Satan had his companions, fellow devils, to admire and encourage him, but I am solitary and abhorred" (15). The monster is, he finds, no more a Satan than he is an Adam: "He had come forth from the hands of God a perfect creature, happy and prosperous, guarded by the especial care of his Creator"; "God, in pity, made man beautiful and alluring, after his own image; but my form is a filthy type of yours, more horrid even from the very resemblance" (15).

The truth, in fact, is that the creature *most* resembles his creator precisely in not fitting any prototype, in not having a settled role in a preordained universe. For Victor, too, is first Adam – blessed with an Edenic childhood, a nurturing parent, and (in his cousin Elizabeth) an Eve; then he is God, the master-creator whose new species will "bless" him as its father; and now he is Satan, the killer of innocence – "I, the true murderer... bore a hell within me that nothing could extinguish" (8) – who has unleashed upon the world a monster of sin made in the image of "the fiend that lurked in my heart" (9).

Moreover, in what Muriel Spark called the dance of mutual pursuit, rage and revenge which absorbs the final chapters of the book ("a sort of figure-of-eight *macarabesque,* executed by two partners moving with the virtuosity of ice-skaters"), the interchangeability and reversals of victim and persecutor, aggrieved and aggressor, produce an ever more complex and inseparable tangle of identities, of good and evil, love and hate. "There is great good and great evil, but which is really which?"

For some influential critics, this moral uncertainty is central to the work's enduring power. All the protagonists, say Gilbert and Gubar, appear, like Mary Shelley herself, "to be trying to understand their presence in a fallen world, and trying at the same time to define the precise nature of the lost paradise that must have preceded the Fall. But unlike Adam, all three characters seem to have fallen not merely from Eden but from the Earth, fallen directly to Hell, like Sin and Satan".

This sense of generalised fallenness is compounded by a shared sense of guilt which stretches beyond the central protagonists (Justine, for example, confesses to William's murder even though she is wholly innocent). It is as if the world of the novel were indeed infected by original sin.

Moreover, characters who are otherwise very different such as Justine, Felix, Elizabeth, Safie, Victor, Walton and the monster, share a common orphanhood. The monster's central questions – "Who was I? What was I? Whence did I come? What was my destination?" (15) (which are themselves a parody of Adam's wondering in paradise, "who was I, or where, or from what cause/[I] knew not" in Book Eight of *Paradise Lost*) – belong, on

A "HORROR STORY OF MATERNITY"

"It is of course open to any of us to claim that Mary Shelley's story is *really* about the unconscious and ultimately about her own," says Marilyn Butler. For feminist critics especially, Mary Shelley's unconscious is most powerfully at work in what Ellen Moers calls the novel's "revulsion against newborn life". Anne Mellor goes so far as to say that the events of the novel – "exactly nine months enwomb the telling of the history of Frankenstein" – not only correspond with one of Mary Shelley's pregnancies, but "exactly mirror the dates of Mary Shelley's own conception and birth", and the death, from postpartum fever, of her mother, ten days later.

Mary Shelley's journal and letters for the period before and during the writing of

some level, to all of them. So, increasingly, as knowledge and experience cause him to suffer, does the monster's anguish grow at being "cast abroad" (16) without succour or guide. Lowry Nelson writes:

> The universe of *Frankenstein* is almost frighteningly without God or devil; the God of conventional fiction, even a tyrant God, has effectually disappeared, just as the devil of earlier gothic diabolism has disappeared as the archfiend. In a universe without the presence of divine justice or retribution, notions of good and evil lose their simple polarity and generate shadowy and expected polarities.

Frankenstein certainly unfold the following grim chronology:

1814 Mary, 16 and pregnant with Shelley's child, elopes with him in July, accompanied by Mary's step-sister, Claire. Mary's father, William Godwin, disowns his daughter. Shelley's legal wife, Harriet, also pregnant, gives birth to a son in November.

1815 A daughter is born to Mary, prematurely, and dies in March. ("Find my baby dead," her Journal notes, "A miserable day"; "Dream that my little baby came to life again; that it had only been cold, and that we rubbed it before the fire, and it lived.") In April, she is pregnant again.

1816 A son, William, is born in January. (Dies in 1819.) Mary begins writing *Frankenstein* in June. In October, Mary's half-sister, Fanny Imlay (the illegitimate daughter of Mary Wollstonecraft) commits suicide feeling abandoned by her siblings. In early December, Mary is pregnant again. In mid-

The novel's modernity, concludes George Levine, lies "in its transformation of traditional Christian and pagan myths into unremitting secularity, into the myth of mankind as it must work within the limits of the visible, physical world".

Is *Frankenstein* a feminist novel?

According to Diane Long Hoeveller, *Frankenstein* may be more important in the development of feminist literary theory than any other novel. "All the interesting, complex characters in the book are

December, Harriet Shelley (pregnant with another's man's child) drowns herself in the Serpentine.

1817 In January, Claire gives birth to her own illegitimate child, Allegra, by Byron. (Allegra dies, 1822.) Percy Shelley is denied custody of his two children, Ianthe and Charles, by Harriet, on the grounds that his abandonment of his wife and his athiestical views make him an unfit father. The Shelleys arrange for publication of *Frankenstein* in May, and Mary

gives birth to their daughter, Clara, in September. (Clara dies 1818, following an impetuous trip to Venice.)

By the time of Percy Shelley's death (in violent storms off the coast of Italy in 1822), not only Allegra, but three of Mary and Percy's children, have died: only Percy Florence, born 1819, survives.

In her famous and ground-breaking feminist study of *Frankenstein,* Ellen Moers wrote of this "horror story of maternity":

male," says Barbara Johnson, "and their deepest attachments are to other males. The females, on the other hand, are beautiful, gentle, selfless, boring nurturers and victims who never experience inner conflict or true desire."

Yet understanding the way women are portrayed in *Frankenstein* is crucial to understanding the novel. In one landmark feminist reading in the 1970s, Ellen Moers saw it as a "birth myth", a frightening vision – or "phantasmagoria" of "the nursery" in which Mary Shelley atones for, or expiates, the guilt she feels about "causing" her mother's death and about her failure to produce an heir for her husband. (Between the ages of 16 and 21, Mary Shelley was almost unceasingly pregnant,

Death and birth were as hideously intermixed in the life of Mary Shelley as in Frankenstein's "filthy workshop of creation"... [Mary] was an unwed mother, responsible for breaking up a marriage of a young woman just as much a mother as she. The father whom she adored broke furiously with her when she eloped; and Mary Wollstonecraft, the mother whose memory she revered, and whose books she was re-reading throughout her teenage years, had died in childbirth – died giving birth to Mary herself. Surely no outside influence need be sought to explain Mary Shelley's fantasy of the new-born as at once monstrous agent of destruction and piteous victim of parental abandonment... The sources of this Gothic conception... were surely the anxieties of a woman who, as daughter, mistress and mother, was bearer of death. ∎

had several miscarriages and lost three of the four children to whom she gave birth.) This view of the novel as expressing Mary Shelley's "revulsion of newborn life" led to an explosion of feminist interest in the novel in the 1980s. To Barbara Johnson, for example, *Frankenstein* is, in part, an "unsettling formulation of the relation between parenthood and monstrousness... a study of post-partum depression... a representation of maternal rejection of a newborn infant".

For Johnson, as for Mary Poovey, however, Shelley's horror of maternal creativity is closely intertwined with a recoil from her own act of artistic creation. In her 1831 Preface to the novel, Mary Shelley wrote of the "dream" which produced the tale:

> I saw the pale student of unhallowed arts
> kneeling beside the thing he had put together. I
> saw the hideous phantasm of a man stretched out,
> and then, on the working of some powerful
> engine, show signs of life, and stir with an uneasy,
> half vital motion. Frightful must it be; for
> supremely frightful would be the effect of any
> endeavour to mock the stupendous mechanism of
> the Creator of the world. His success would
> terrify the artist; he would rush away from his
> odious handywork, horror-stricken. He would
> hope that, left to itself, the slight spark of life
> which he had communicated would fade; that this
> thing, which had received such imperfect

animation, would subside into dead matter; and
he might sleep in the belief that the silence of the
grave would quench forever the transient
existence of the hideous corpse which he had
looked upon as the cradle of life. He sleeps; but
he is awakened; he opens his eyes; behold the
horrid thing stands at his bedside, opening his
curtains, and looking on him with yellow, watery,
but speculative eyes.

For Poovey, this statement of "how the monster's
creator, now referred to specifically as an artist,
transgresses the grounds of propriety through his
art" expresses powerfully Mary Shelley's own guilt
at being, impermissibly, both woman/mother and
artist at once.

In the thematic emphasis of the novel, Shelley
expresses the tension she felt between the
self-denial demanded by domestic activity and
the self-assertiveness essential to artistic
creation... She finds literary production to be a
perverse substitute for woman's natural function:
a "hideous corpse" usurps what should be the
"cradle of life"... As Mary Shelley imagines her
female self, she gives her own conflicted energy
the form of a monster.

Shelley's 1831 Preface ends with the words: "And
now, once again, I bid my hideous progeny go forth
and prosper." It is a significant sentence, as Sandra

Gilbert and Susan Gubar argue in their ground-breaking study, *The Madwoman in the Attic* (1979). Not only does the sentence link Victor's creation with Shelley's. It also makes plain the author's "anxiety about her own aesthetic activity", implying that "in her alienated attic workshop of filthy creation she has given birth to a deformed book, a literary abortion or miscarriage".

Gilbert and Gubar also suggest that *Frankenstein* is a woman's re-reading and re-writing of Milton's *Paradise Lost* in which "both Victor and his monster" play the neo-biblical parts – not only those of Adam and Satan, but also Eve. Franken-stein's "single most self-defining act", after all, is that of procreation – "Victor Frankenstein has a baby" – and this "transforms him definitively into Eve", especially since the central transgressive act involves his eating, like the first woman and mother, from the forbidden tree of knowledge.

> Not Adam but Eve, not Satan but Sin, not male but female, [what Frankenstein] really enacts is the story of Eve's discovery not that she must fall but that, having been created female, she *is fallen,* femaleness and fallenness being essentially synonymous.

But the monster, too, think Gilbert and Gubar, is "a female in disguise"; marginalised by society, his narrative is "a philosophical meditation on what it means to be born without a soul or history, as well as an exploration of what it feels like to be a 'filthy mass that moves and talks', a thing, an other, a creature of the second sex". In his "shuddering sense of deformity" – as in "his namelessness and his orphaned motherless isolation" – the monster resembles most closely the Eve who was "made in the image of a male creator" and whose "unprecedented femininity" seemed merely "a defective masculinity, a deformity":

> *Accursed creator! Why did you form a monster so hideous that even you turned from me in disgust? My form is but a filthy type of yours.* (15)

Mary Shelley retells the story of the Fall, conclude Gilbert and Gubar, "not so much to protest against it, as to clarify its [misogynistic] meaning".

Mary Jacobus's study of *Frankenstein* also regards it as a "bizarre parody of the Fall" but her emphasis is on how women in the novel are, nonetheless, a major problem for the monster:

> A curious thread in the plot focuses not on the image of the hostile father (Frankenstein/God) but on the dead mother who comes to symbolize to the monster his loveless state. Literally unmothered, he fantasises acceptance by a series of women but founders in imagined rebuffs and ends in silence... On Justine's person the monster wreaks his revenge on all women, planting among her clothes the incriminating

evidence of the mother's portrait as the supposed motive for the murder of the little boy. She is duly tried and executed, even confessing to the crime – for in the monstrous logic of the text, she is as guilty as the monster claims: "The crime had its source in her: be hers the punishment." Eve is to blame for having been desired.

By the same "monstrous logic", Jacobus argues, if woman is the cause of the monster's crimes, then the only cure for the monster is a mate "as hideous as myself" (17). But Mary Shelley no more than

EDUCATION IN THE NOVEL

"I believe we are sent here to educate ourselves," wrote Mary Shelley in her Journal.

All three of the central protagonists of *Frankenstein* are essentially self-educated. "My education was neglected," Walton writes in Letter 1, and in Letter 2 describes himself as, at 28, "more illiterate than many schoolboys of fifteen." "Yet I was passionately fond of reading... For the first fourteen years of my life, I ran wild on a common and read nothing but my Uncle Thomas's books of voyages." Frankenstein, too, says: "I was to a great degree self-taught with regard to my favourite studies. My father was not scientific, and I was left to struggle with a child's blindness, added to a student's thirst for knowledge" (2). And, of course, the monster's knowledge of human history and progress is mediated entirely by the books he finds and studiously reads at the de Lacey cottage (15).

The protagonists all share William Godwin's belief that a child is best educated by finding his or her own way to enlightenment. Political justice

Frankenstein can bring herself "to embody woman as fully monstrous", because, as Barbara Johnson puts it: "Monstrousness is incompatible with femininity."

For Anne Mellor, it is Frankenstein's scientific project itself which carries the novel's central feminist message: the ambition to "become the sole creator of a human being" supports a "patriarchal denial" of the value of women and female sexuality:

> By stealing the female's control over reproduction, Frankenstein has eliminated the female's primary biological function and source of cultural power.

meant, for Godwin, one system or school that educates teacher and pupil, parent and child alike in the exercise of reason – a democratic vision which overturned the conventional hierarchical model of learning.

In *Frankenstein*, Walton's youth is spent under the "gentle and feminine fosterage" of his sister (Letter 2). The gentleness and mutual respect of the de Laceys impels the creature to learn to read and speak in order that he can "join" their world. Frankenstein's parents, "possessed by the spirit of kindness" were "not the tyrants to rule our lot according to their caprice, but the agents and creators of all the many delights which we enjoyed... gratitude assisted the development of filial love" (2).

Moreover, in important ways, too, the educational experiences of her protagonists repeat Mary Shelley's own. Her intellect was shaped by Godwin's influence and guidance, and, despite the loss of personal contact after her elopement with Percy Shelley, Mary continued the regime of daily study established by her father, mixing literary works with politics, science and history and re-reading, in the year before she wrote *Frankenstein*, the books found by the monster – *The Sorrows of Werther, Plutarch's Lives,* and *Paradise Lost.* ∎

Indeed, for the simple purpose of human survival, Frankenstein has eliminated the necessity to have females at all. One of the deepest horrors of this novel is Frankenstein's implicit goal of creating a society for men only; his creature male, he refuses to create a female; there is no reason that the race of mortal beings he hoped to propagate should not be exclusively male.

Recent feminist criticism, however, concentrates largely on the exclusively male cast of characters. In the early 1990s, for example, Bette London read *Frankenstein* as a novel concerned with the "production of masculinity", with "the troubled and troubling representation of the male body" – with, in short, "man-making". Frankenstein sets out to create the perfect man according to an ideal masculine prototype. The incoherent and monstrous being he assembles discloses how patriarchal conventions of masculinity are disastrous distortions of maleness as it is individually experienced. The novel suggests that

masculinity as much as femininity is created by cultural negotiations and contestations. It insists that brokenness has no necessary or exclusive connection to the feminine – witness Frankenstein's self-exhibition as "a miserable spectacle of wrecked humanity".

Frankenstein's "dreadful secret", London suggests, is "the repression of masculine contradiction". In these later feminist readings, then, Victor Frankenstein is understood not so much as a *perpetrator* of patriarchal oppression of women but as a *victim*, himself subject to the pressure of coercive social norms which, in demanding conformity, produce damage, fragmentation and deformity.

Moreover, when Frankenstein says to Walton before embarking on his narrative "I once had a friend, the most noble of human creatures, and am entitled, therefore, to judge respecting friendship", he is referring not to Elizabeth but to Henry Clerval. Does this suggest that the only real friendships are male ones, in opposition to the feminine sphere, or is it, on the other hand, a model of what Mary Wollstonecraft called "a nutritive relationship between two human beings" (the maleness or femaleness of the individuals in question being irrelevant)? This type of mutually enriching relationship between equals is, of course, the ideal which Wollstonecraft (and indeed William Godwin) originally envisaged.

What makes *Frankenstein* such an extraordinary achievement?

Why, finally, does *Frankenstein* matter? What is its intrinsic achievement, aside from its being a myth endlessly appropriated for others' political, philosophical or ethical purposes?

What impresses most about the novel, perhaps, is this. A young, inexperienced woman of 18 bravely bit off more than she – perhaps more than anyone – could really chew. In the face of her timidity, her fear of failing her literary-intellectual family, her sense of littleness and non-entitlement, she went for the big idea, the giant leap of imaginative endeavour. This book is that rare thing, a true original. Such an accomplishment would be extraordinary in any lifetime. That Mary Shelley brought it off when she was barely an adult is truly astonishing.

But what lies behind this creative feat – and what also startles – is a profound seriousness about existence. It wasn't a conventional intellectual seriousness inherited or imbibed from her parents. Its source was an involuntary attunement to the deep trouble and inherent sorrow of human experience – a capacity to hear it and feel it as well as be its witness. This is a writer's seriousness, and it is the chief ground upon which Mary Shelley deserves to be taken seriously as a writer.

Take the deep centre of this book – the monster's tale. There is no more moving instance in 19th-century English fiction of the drama of fallenness – of how ill-fitted human creatures are to the world they occupy, how terrible is the necessary separation into individuality, of how alone we all are. This narrative of loneliness and loss cries out, like King Lear: "Who is it that can tell me who I am?" There is no more memorable cautionary tale of how hell is not elsewhere but here and now, and how humans – cruelly if inadvertently – can help make it so. Mary Shelley risked everything – failure, ridicule, (female) reputation, humiliation – to make what is painful and irremediable in experience as unforgettably 'horrid' as possible. That is why, 200 years after its composition, *Frankenstein* still has so much so powerfully to say to us.

MARY SHELLEY'S FAMILY CIRCLE

> It is not singular that, as the daughter of two
> persons of distinguished literary celebrity, I should
> very early in life have thought of writing... My
> husband... was from the first very anxious that I
> should prove myself worthy of my parentage and
> enroll myself on the page of fame.
>   (Mary Shelley, 1831 Preface to *Frankenstein*)

William Godwin (1756–1836)

Mary Shelley's father was an ex-Dissenting minister
turned atheist and radical political thinker whose most
famous work, *Enquiry Concerning Political Justice*,
published in 1793, just after the French Revolution, made
him an overnight celebrity. Godwin, said the Romantic
writer and critic, William Hazlitt, "blazed as a sun in the
firmament of reputation". "Throw aside your books of
chemistry," Wordsworth told a young student, "and read
Godwin on necessity."

The basic argument of *Political Justice* is that human
beings are perfectible. They achieve full humanity when
they are aware of their power of choice and capable of
using it through free exercise of reason. Their imperfect
state is largely the fault of repressive social institutions
and artificial restraints.

Thus Godwin argued for the dissolution of
government. The unfair hierarchical structure of society,
based on property, privilege and oppressive law, should be
replaced by a just and equal society, based on community

of interest. The individual who passively obeyed authority and custom (including the convention of marriage) was the victim of mere superstition, no more reasonable than an animal.

Godwin's fame was short-lived, however. He lost credibility in the backlash against the terror unleashed by the French revolution in the mid-1790s, sinking into virtual obscurity until his ideas were rediscovered in 1812 by Percy Bysshe Shelley, the brilliant young poet (and his daughter's future husband), who became his benefactor as well as his champion.

In later life, Mary wrote of an "excessive and romantic attachment to my father": "Until I met Shelley, I could justly say that he was my God." Godwin described his own demeanour toward his daughter as "sententious and authoritative". The distance in their emotional relationship was not helped by widower Godwin's remarriage, when Mary was four. "I detest Mrs G," she wrote at the age of 17; "she plagues my father out of his life." The new Mrs Godwin's conventional expectations of the household were wholly out of keeping with her father's own: "I was nursed and fed with a love of glory. To be something great and good was the precept given me by my Father: Shelley reiterated it."

For the first bold step which Mary took, however – the elopement with her father's young and passionate prodigy, Percy Shelley, which actually put into practice Godwin's own theoretical rejection of the institution of marriage – her father never forgave her. He summarily cut her out of his life, even while continuing to accept Shelley's financial help (a responsibility which, after Shelley's father withheld his allowance, was no inconsiderable burden to the young outcast couple).

No less vexed than their personal relationship is that of Mary Shelley's novel to her father's ideas. Versed in his work from an early age, she re-read *Political Justice* only the year before *Frankenstein* was written, and dedicated the first edition to him. But is the novel a tribute to Godwin's views or a critique of them? It can be read as either, or both.

What is not in doubt is the influence on *Frankenstein* of Godwin's own fictional writings, especially his most popular novel, *The Adventures of Caleb Williams*, published in 1799. A nightmare "Gothic" novel of persecution, it is the model for the charged sequence of encounter and flight enacted by Frankenstein and the monster amid the otherworldly shadowlands of glacial isolation.

Mary Wollstonecraft (1759–1797)

Like her husband, Wollstonecraft was inspired by the possibilities of real political change which the French revolution appeared to promise. But her writings were all the more strikingly radical for being *about* women and *by* a woman whose life was as courageously unconventional as her thinking.

Her *Memoirs*, which Godwin published in 1798 after his wife's death, outraged the public by their candid account of her love affair with a married man (Anglo-Swiss painter, Henry Fuseli), her liaison with American Gilbert Imlay (with whom she had a child, Fanny), her two attempts at suicide when Imlay was unfaithful, and her residence in revolutionary France after she had travelled alone to Paris. When Mary Godwin eloped with Percy Bysshe Shelley at the age of 16, the couple felt justified not only by Godwin's treatise against marriage in *Political Justice* but by the example of Wollstonecraft's own emancipated personal and sexual life.

Her most famous work, *A Vindication of the Rights of Woman* (1792), was a passionate feminist plea for women's rights, based on the ideals she shared with Godwin. Not only were the rights and potential of women equivalent to those of men; the oppression and enslavement of women corrupted both sexes. Moreover, social progress was impossible if one half of society was subject to the vice and misery of ignorance by being barred from all opportunity for enlightenment. Education was critical to the accomplishment of this vision.

> Not only the virtue, but the *knowledge* of the two sexes should be the same in nature, if not in degree, and [women] considered not only as moral, but rational creatures ought to endeavor to acquire human virtues (or perfections) by the *same* means as men, instead of being educated like a sensible kind of *half* being.

Frankenstein's monster, feminist critics argue – a type of "*half* being" – is an image of the female degradation that *A Vindication of the Rights of Woman* depicts. There are strong grounds for the contention that *Frankenstein* continues Wollstonecraft's work of giving voice and external form to the hidden yet universal injuries and injustices of female experience.

Mary Wollstonecraft and William Godwin didn't live up to their own radical views, however. In March 1797, when Mary discovered she was pregnant with William's child, they immediately got married. When Mary gave birth to a daughter, also named Mary, in August of that year, she fell ill with puerperal poisoning, and died 10 days later. The only intimate knowledge that Mary Shelley was to have of her mother was through reading her journals and books, which she did compulsively through her teenage years, by her graveside.

Percy Bysshe Shelley (1792–1822)

The son of a baronet, and conventionally educated at Eton and Oxford, Shelley had early shown signs of his rebellious, eccentric genius. He had privately published fiction and verse in his teens, including *Original Poetry by Victor and Cazire* in 1810, with his sister, Elizabeth (names which are duplicated in the Victor-Elizabeth relationship in *Frankenstein*), and was an ardent experimenter. He was dubbed "mad Shelley" and the "Eton atheist" by his peers, and forced to leave Oxford after circulating a pamphlet, *The Necessity of Atheism.* He broke permanently with his family when he eloped in 1811 with the 16-year-old Harriet Westbrook.

From 1812, the 19-year-old Percy became a frequent visitor to the Godwin household, declaring his revolutionary utopian fantasy, *Queen Mab* (1813), a translation into verse of *The Enquiry Concerning Political Justice* and claiming Godwin as his philosophical parent-mentor. A passionate, eloquent and reverent disciple, Percy was soon also attached to Godwin's daughter, Mary:

"I do not think there is an excellence at which human nature can arrive, that she does not indisputably possess... So intimately are our natures now united that I feel whilst I describe her excellencies as if I were an egoist expatiating upon his own perfections."

In 1814, Percy eloped with Mary, then 16, and her stepsister Claire Claremont, setting up not merely a ménage à trois, but an extended erotic community comprising, among other Romantic figures, Byron and Thomas Hogg (between Mary and whom, Shelley amicably encouraged an amorous correspondence). This was the prelude to Percy Shelley's major creative period, when he produced, among other great works, *Prometheus Unbound*. But the beautiful non-political "Alastor or The Spirit of Solitude" is the poem which first gained public admiration for Shelley. Appearing in 1816, its account of the pursuit of truth in unnatural isolation anticipates Frankenstein's own obsessive seeking (depicted by Mary Shelley in the same year): "I have made my bed/ In charnels and on coffins ... Hoping to still these obstinate questionings ... Of what we are".

When Mary Shelley began composing *Frankenstein* by the shores of Lake Geneva, and Byron wrote his epic of Romantic verse-drama *Manfred*, Shelley was writing "Mont Blanc", his meditative ode on the relative power of the imagination and of nature in a secular world, the influence of which scene and thought is palpable in Chapter 10 of *Frankenstein*.

But the losses of this period were profound. Mary and Percy's first daughter died at a few days old in 1814. In October 1816, Mary's half-sister, Fanny Imlay, committed suicide and in December 1816, Percy's first wife, Harriet, took her own life. Over the next six years, Mary and Percy would lose two more children and Mary would suffer miscarriages. The couple became increasingly estranged, and Mary was often alone and depressed. Shelley was drowned in violent storms off the coast of Italy in 1822.

In later life, Mary Shelley said of the couple's youthful experiment in living: "it was acting a novel, being an incarnate romance". Shelley's poetry was famously impractical even to his own generation – "a passionate dream," said Hazlitt, "a striving after impossibilities, a record of fond conjectures, of vague abstraction – a fever of the soul... indulging its love of power and novelty at the expense of truth and nature".

For some critics, *Frankenstein* challenges the whole Romantic myth of the Promethean creator – brilliant, ambitious, passionate, yet obsessive, self-centred and ultimately destructive. "Through the mouth of her hero," says Robert Kiely, "she raises a question which in life she could probably never bring herself to ask her husband: 'Is genius forever separable from the reasonable the reflective, the probable?'"

"It would hardly be surprising," said Peter Dale Scott in "Mary, Percy and the Psycho-political Integrity of *Frankenstein,* "if Mary had simply resented Percy as an ideological Prometheus with herself as the victim." Instead, he says, *Frankenstein*, written when the couple were still close,

does not simply contrast their personalities [Romantic male intellectual ambition versus suffering female domestic sentiment] but also fuses them: there are aspects of Mary in the overly masculine Victor, as well as of both Mary and Percy in the suffering daemon. This was possible because in essentials Mary and Percy were one.

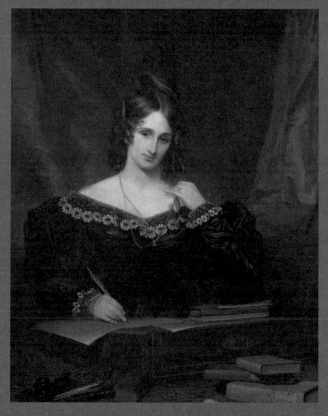

Mary Wollstonecraft Shelley (1797 - 1851)

WHAT THE CRITICS SAY

"*[Frankenstein]* is one of the most original and
complete productions of the day. We debate with
ourselves in wonder as we read it, what could have been
the series of thoughts – what could have been the
peculiar experiences that awakened them – which
conduced in the author's mind, to the astonishing
combinations of motives and incidents, and the
startling catastrophe which compose this tale."

Percy Bysshe Shelley, 1818

"Our taste and our judgement alike revolt at this kind of
writing, and the greater the ability with which it may be
executed the worse it is. It inculcates no lesson of
conduct, manners, or morality... it fatigues the feelings
without interesting the understanding: it gratuitously
harasses the heart, and only adds to the store, already
too great of painful sensation... the reader [is left] after
a struggle between laughter and loathing, in doubt
whether the head or the heart of the author be most
diseased."

The Quarterly Review, 1818

"Perhaps the foulest toadstool that has yet sprung up
from the reeking dunghill of the present times."

William Beckford,
author of the 1786 Gothic novel, *Vathek*

"Upon the whole, the work impresses us with a high idea of the author's original genius and happy power of [exciting] new reflections and untried sources of emotion. [If] Paradise [is] to lie on a couch and read new novels... no small praise is due to him, who, like the author of Frankenstein, has enlarged the sphere of that fascinating enjoyment."

Sir Walter Scott, 1818

"For a man it was excellent, but for a woman it was wonderful."

Blackwood's Edinburgh Magazine, 1823

"Methinks it is a wonderful work for a girl of nineteen – *not* nineteen, indeed, at that time."

Lord Byron

"Perhaps the wonder of it exists, not despite Mary's youth, but because of it. *Frankenstein* is Mary Shelley's best novel, because at that early age she was not well acquainted with her own mind."

Muriel Spark, 1951

"To say flatly that the Monster is Frankenstein's id on the rampage and that he subconsciously desires his family's extermination would be pretentious and anachronistic... It is quite different to argue that Frankenstein and his Monster have much in common, that they are objectified parts of a single sensibility, and that they represent the intimate good and bad struggle in the human personality. Evil is within, in one's own works and creations.

Lowry Nelson, 1963

"Mary Shelley's *Frankenstein* made the Gothic novel over into what today we call science fiction. *Frankenstein* brought a new sophistication to literary terror and it did so without a heroine, without even an important female victim. Paradoxically, however, no other Gothic work by a woman writer, perhaps no literary work of any kind by a woman, better repays examination in the light of the sex of its author."

Ellen Moers, 1977

"'Frankenstein' became an entry in every serious recent dictionary by way of the variations – dramas, films, television versions – through which Mary Shelley's monster and his creator most obviously survive. But while *Frankenstein* is a phenomenon of Western culture, it is so because it has tapped into the centre of Western feeling and imagination... *Frankenstein* has become a metaphor for our own cultural crises."

George Levine, 1979

A SHORT CHRONOLOGY

1797 Mary born on August 30. Her mother, Mary Wollstonecraft, dies on September 10.

1812 First meeting with Percy Shelley.

1814 Elopes with Shelley to the Continent.

1815 In February, Mary gives birth prematurely to a baby girl in February who dies in March.

1816 Mary gives birth to a son, William, in January. She, Percy and her step-sister Claire travel to Geneva in May to live near Byron (with whose child Claire is pregnant). In June and July, they visit Mont Blanc and Mary begins *Frankenstein*. In September, Mary, Percy and Claire return to England and settle in Bath, where Mary continues with *Frankenstein*. In October, Mary's half-sister commits suicide. Mary and Percy marry in London on December 30th.

1818 *Frankenstein* published anonymously.

1822 Percy Shelley dies at sea.

1823 Mary publishes her second novel, *Valperga*.

1824 Mary publishes her edition of Percy Shelley's *Posthumous Poems*.

1836 Mary's father, William Godwin, dies.

1851 Mary dies of a brain tumour and is buried with her parents.

FURTHER READING

Graham Allen, *Mary Shelley: Critical Issues* (Basingstoke: Palgrave Macmillan, 2008).

Chris Baldick, *In Frankenstein's Shadow: Myth, Monstrosity, and Nineteenth-Century Writing* (Oxford: Clarendon Press, 1996).

Harold Bloom, *Mary Shelley: Modern Critical Views* (New York: Chelsea House Publishers, 1985).

Fred Botting, *Making Monstrous: Frankenstein, criticism, theory* (Manchester: Manchester University Press, 1991).

Marilyn Butler, *Romantics, Rebels and Reactionaries: English Literature and its Background; 1760-1830* (Oxford: Oxford University Press, 1981).

Pamela Clemit, *The Godwinian Novel The Rational Fictions of Godwin, Brockden Brown, Mary Shelley* (Oxford: Clarendon Press, 1983).

Kate Ellis, *The Contested Castle: Gothic Novels and the Subversion of Domestic Ideology* (Chicago: University of Illinois, 1989).

Sandra M. Gilbert and Susan Gubar, *The Madwoman in the Attic: The Woman Writer and the Nineteenth-Century Literary Imagination* (New Haven and London: Yale University Press, 1979).

Rosemary Jackson, *Fantasy: The Literature of Subversion* (London and New York: Methuen, 1981)

Mary Jacobus, *Is There a Woman in This Text? New Literary History*, 14 (1982) 117-41.

Robert Kiely, *The Romantic Novel in England* (Cambridge, Mass.: Harvard University Press, 1972).

George Levine and U. C. Knoepflmacher, *The Endurance of Frankenstein* (Berkeley: University of California Press, 1979).

Robert Miles, *Gothic Writing 1750-1820: A Genealogy* (Manchester: Manchester University Press, 2002).

Ellen Moers, *Literary Women* (London: The Women's Press, 1978).

Timothy Morton (ed), *Mary Shelley's Frankenstein: A Sourcebook* (London and New York: Routledge, 2002).

Paul Sherwin, 'Frankenstein: Creation as Catastrophe', *Modern Language Association* 96:5 (Oct. 1981)

Mary Poovey, *The Proper Lady and the Woman Writer* (Chicago: Chicago University Press, 1984).

David Punter, *The Literature of Terror: A History of Gothic Fictions from 1865 to the Present Day* (London: Longman, 1980).

Muriel Spark, *Child Of Light* (London: Tower Bridge Publications, 1951).

Notes

Notes

Notes

Notes

INDEX

First published in 2016 by
Connell Guides
Artist House
35 Little Russell Street
London WC1A 2HH

10 9 8 7 6 5 4 3 2 1

Copyright © Connell Guides Publishing Ltd.
All rights reserved. No part of this publication
may be reproduced, stored in a retrieval system or transmitted in any
form, or by any means (electronic, mechanical, or otherwise) without
the prior written permission of both the copyright owners
and the publisher.

Picture credits:
p.17 © Print Collector / Hulton Archive / Getty Images
p.41 © Moviestore / REX / Shutterstock
p.57 © Everett / REX / Shutterstock
p.79 © Moviestore / REX / Shutterstock
p.113 © Heritage Images / Hulton Archive / Getty Images

A CIP catalogue record for this book is available from the British Library.
ISBN 978-1-907776-57-1

Design © Nathan Burton

Assistant Editor and typeset by:
Brian Scrivener and Paul Woodward

Printed in Great Britain by
Bell and Bain Ltd, Glasgow

www.connellguides.com